World Cup '94

Keir Radnedge

HAMLYN

Contents

PICTURE ACKNOWLEDGEMENTS

Allsport 5 (inset), 15, 20 (centre inset), 24-5 (main picture), 47 top, 62-3, Shaun Botterill 27 bottom left, 28 bottom, 30 bottom left, 31 centre, 41 top right and bottom, 48, 49, 51 bottom, 55 bottom, Clive Brunskill 1 (right inset), 26 top and bottom, 39, 40 top and bottom, 56 top left, Simon Bruty 19, 54 bottom right, David Cannon 1 (main picture and centre inset), 5 (main picture), 20-1 (main picture), 21 (top inset), 27 bottom right, 33, 34 top, 42 top, 50 top and bottom, 56 bottom, 57 top right and bottom right, 58 centre, 60 bottom, Jim Commentucci 60 top left, Jonathan Daniel 61 bottom, S. Halleran 60 top right, Mike Hewitt 47 bottom, 58 top, Bill Hickey 2-3, Inpho 43 bottom, 55 top left, Michael King 18, Ken Levine 61 top, Cor Mooy 17, Steve Morton 55 top right, 59 top and bottom, Ben Radford 22 (bottom left inset), 30 top and bottom right, 35 top and bottom, 37, 46 top and bottom, 52 top and bottom, 54 bottom left, 59 centre, Pascal Rondeau 32 top and bottom, Dan Smith 34 bottom left, 38, Bill Stickland 25 (top inset), Vandystadt 1 (left inset); Colorsport 16, 20 (top and bottom insets), 21 (centre and bottom insets), 22-3 (main picture), 22 (top left, top right and bottom right insets), 23 (top and bottom insets), 24 (all four insets), 25 (bottom left and bottom right insets), 27 top and centre, 28 top, 29 left and right, 31 top and bottom, 34 bottom right, 36 top and bottom, 41 top left, 42 bottom, 43 top, 44, 44-5 top and bottom, 51 top, 53, 54 top, 56 top right, 57 top left and bottom left, Olympia 56 centre, 58 bottom; FIFA 6, 8, 10, 11; Hill and Knowlton (UK), Ltd/Questra 4 et passim (official World Cup 1994 ball); Hulton Deutsch Collection 7, 12, 13; Press Association/Reuter 9; Syndication International 14.

First published in Great Britain in 1994 by Hamlyn an imprint of Reed Consumer Books Limited
Michelin House, 81 Fulham Road, London SW3 6RB and Auckland, Melbourne, Singapore and Toronto

Copyright © 1994 Reed International Books Limited

ISBN 0 600 58320 1

A catalogue record for this book is available from the British Library

Printed in Spain

Introduction

THE WORLD CUP is the pinnacle of achievement for any footballer. I know: I was there with the Republic of Ireland four years ago in Italy and I hope to be there again in the United States.

The choice of host nation promises to make it the most exciting World Cup tournament in the event's 64-year history. But I wonder quite whether the Americans know exactly what is going to hit them – from Brazil's Samba-dancing fans to the Dutch orchestras. And that's before the football even starts!

We all know that England, Scotland, Wales and Northern Ireland will not be there. I feel desperately sorry for the players and for fans who had spent the best part of the last four years dreaming of following their favourites all the way to New York and right across America to Dallas, Chicago, Los Angeles and all those other fabulous host cities.

I was fortunate enough to play with the Irish Republic at a US Cup tournament with the Americans, Italy and Portugal two years ago. The atmosphere was electric, the facilities tremendous. Anyone who goes – player or fan – will have no excuse for not enjoying themselves.

A lot of people opposed the nomination of the United States as World Cup hosts because the country had no soccer pedigree. Those were people who didn't know that the Americans reached the semi-finals of the very first World Cup in Uruguay way back in 1930. Also, I seem to recall, the Americans once beat England in the World Cup . . .

The truth of the matter is that the World Cup is such a huge event, both commercially and technologically, that only a handful of countries are now capable of staging it. Clearly, when it comes to those qualities, the United States has a head start.

But the Americans also know how to enjoy themselves. They are sports fanatics. Forget all the suggestions that they will turn out only for baseball or gridiron. Did you know that both one of the semi-finals and then the Final of the football event at the Los Angeles Olympic Games pulled crowds of more than 100,000 apiece?

Those matches were staged in Pasadena, where the Final of the 1994 World Cup will be staged in the Rosebowl on July 17.

Long before then you will see the Americans turn out in force to support USA '94. It's their World Cup and they will make the most of it. Advance ticket sales have never been as demanding as in the United States last year.

THOUGHTS ON THE DRAW

'No group will be easy,' I thought prior to the draw in Las Vegas. Immediately after the draw there was one reaction throughout Ireland – What did we do to deserve this? No Boston – No 'minnow' nation – Italy again – Mexico in Florida at lunch time – it wasn't what we expected.

Then we looked at J.C. shrugging his shoulders and looking like he'd rather be fishing and we all knew everything would be OK. 'We'll go and surprise a few people,' he said. We immediately forgot about our previous encounters with Italy, we forgot how powerful a soccer nation Mexico is and we forgot all about Norway's demolition of their rivals in England's group. The confidence, momentarily disturbed, came flooding back.

Preparations have had to be altered. Now Jack's Army is trying to make contact with long-lost relatives in New York instead of Boston! What the hell! As our eccentric team physio Mick Byrne would say 'The Green Machine is on the move.'

There's no doubt it's a tremendously difficult group but one thing is certain – we'll put them under pressure!

Niall Quinn (Manchester City and Republic of Ireland)

1930 in URUGUAY

History was made in Uruguay in 1930. Jules Rimet, then the president of football's world governing body, FIFA, had for many years wanted to stage a World Cup tournament.

WORLD CUP FINAL

Uruguay 4
Dorado, Cea, Iriarte, Castro

Argentina 2
Peucelle, Stabile

Montevideo, July 30: 93,000

Uruguay: Ballestreros, Nasazzi, Mascheroni, Andrade, Fernandez, Gestido, Dorado, Scarone, Castro, Cea, Iriarte.

Argentina: Botazzo, Della Torre, Paternoster, J Evaristo, Monti, Suarez, Peucelle, Varallo, Stabile, Ferreyra, M Evaristo.

Tournament leading scorer:
Guillermo Stabile (Argentina) 8 goals.

Since 1896 the Olympic Games soccer tournament had been an unofficial world championship. But as professionalism gained ground in Europe and South America, the amateur Olympics were no longer the right stage.

So FIFA decided to launch the first World Cup in 1930 and Uruguay offered to be the hosts. The Uruguayans were celebrating 100 years of independence and promised not only a vast new stadium but to pay all the expenses of the visiting nations.

Only four European nations decided to undertake the long sea crossing – France, Romania, Yugoslavia and Belgium. It was a Frenchman who made history by scoring the first goal in World Cup history. His name was Lucien Laurent and he scored after 19 minutes of the opening match between France and Mexico.

Only 13 countries competed in this first event which meant one first-round group had four teams and all the others three each. Argentina, Yugoslavia, hosts Uruguay and the USA were the four group winners who went straight on into the semi-finals. Here, South American artistry took over. Argentina thrashed the US 6-1 and Uruguay beat Yugoslavia by a similar score. Inside left Pedro Cea scored a hat-trick.

Thousands of Argentinian fans sailed across the River Plate on the morning of July 30. Hundreds of thousands gathered around radios in Buenos Aires. They were to be disappointed. Argentina led Uruguay 2-1 at half-time but it was the hosts who won the first World Cup after recovering with three second-half goals.

The opening ceremony of the inaugural World Cup took place at the brand-new Centenario stadium in Montevideo which also hosted the final on July 30.

in ITALY

Italy raided South America to launch their own first challenge for the World Cup as dictator Benito Mussolini was determined his favourites should score a massive propaganda triumph.

1934

Team manager Vittorio Pozzo was given a free hand to run and select the team. Pozzo called up three Italian-based Argentines in wingers Guaita and Orsi and rough, tough centre-half Luisito Monti – who had been a World Cup runner-up with Argentina four years earlier.

Uruguay, angry that so many European nations had stayed away from 'their' 1930 finals, refused to send a team so it was certain from the outset that a new name would be inscribed on the World Cup.

The format for the finals was changed. In Uruguay in 1930 there had been four first-round mini-leagues. In Italy, however, the World Cup was sudden death knock-out football. Italy opened in dramatic style, thrashing 1930 semi-finalists United States by 7-1. Veteran centre-forward Angelo Schiavio scored a hat-trick.

Other first-round winners included a powerful German side (who beat Belgium 5-2) and Austria, nick-named the Wunderteam, and one of the finest national teams in the history of the game thus far. Austria's star was the centre-forward Matthias Sindelar, nicknamed the Man of Paper he was so slim.

In the quarter-finals Italy needed a replay to win a bruis-ing tie with Spain and they went on to defeat a fading Austria 1-0 in the semi-finals. But Czechoslovakia, in the Final, very nearly caused an upset. Only in extra-time in Rome did the worn-out Schiavio – who could barely run – manage to stab home the winner for Mussolini, Pozzo . . . and Italy.

WORLD CUP FINAL

Italy 2	Czechoslovakia 1
Orsi, Schiavio	Puc
	After extra time

Rome, June 10: 55,000

Italy: Combi, Monzeglio, Allemandi, Ferrari, Monti, Bertolini, Guaita, Meazza, Schiavio, Ferrari, Orsi.

Czechoslovakia: Planicka, Zenisek, Ctyrocky, Kostalek, Cambal, Krcil, Junek, Svoboda, Sobotka, Nejedly, Puc.

Tournament leading scorers:
Schiavio (Italy), Nejedly (Czechoslovakia), Conen (Germany) 4 each.

Vittorio Pozzo, the Italian manager, is carried shoulder-high by his victorious players who had overcome the gifted Czechoslovaks 2-1 after extra-time in the Final.

38 in FRANCE

Italy's manager Vittorio Pozzo rebuilt his team almost entirely, replacing all but the two inside-forwards, Meazza and Ferrari. He had also found a thrilling new centre-forward in Silvio Piola.

WORLD CUP FINAL

Italy 4	Hungary 2
Coloussi 2, Piola 2	Titkos, Sarosi

Paris, June 19: 55,000

Italy: Oliveiri, Foni, Rava, Serantoni, Andreolo, Locatelli, Biavati, Meazza, Piola, Ferrari, Colaussi.

Hungary: Szabo, Polgar, Biro, Szalay, Szucs, Lazar, Sas, Vincze, Sarosi, Zsengeller, Titkos.

Tournament leading scorer:
Leonidas da Silva (Brazil) 8 goals.

The dangers to Italy appeared to be Brazil – with their explosive centre-forward Leonidas – and a German team which included several Austrian stars following Germany's invasion of its south-eastern neighbours earlier that year.

Austria's disappearance from the map of Europe left a gap in the finals line-up. England, though outside FIFA because of a long-standing row over amateurism, were invited to take part at the last minute but refused.

The first round saw the first shock with Germany beaten in a replay by Switzerland who hit back to win 4-2 in extra time after being 2-0 down at half-time. Italy also needed extra time to overcome a plucky Norwegian side 2-1, while Brazil beat Poland 6-5 in an astonishing match which saw both Leonidas and Poland's Ernst Wilimowski scoring four goals apiece.

Czechoslovakia lost their chance of returning to the Final when they lost 2-1 to Brazil in a quarter-final replay. The Czechoslovaks were up against it after goalkeeper Planicka and inside-left Nejedly broke an arm and a leg respectively in the initial 1-1 draw.

Brazil, overconfident, rested stars Leonidas and inside-forward Tim from the semi-final against Italy. They wanted them fresh for the Final, said officials. But they never made it. Italy beat the weakened Brazilians 2-1 in the semi-final in Marseille and went on to dominate Hungary 4-2 in the Final.

Italy (pictured below) outplayed the Hungarians in the Final in Paris to gain a second successive Jules Rimet trophy and add to their 1936 Berlin Olympics gold.

in BRAZIL

Brazil and England were favourites for the first post-war tournament. Brazil had sensational forwards while tournament new-comers England, were legends as founders of the modern game.

1950

Brazil built a huge new stadium, the Maracana, in honour of the World Cup. The stadium was not finished by the time of the opening game in which Brazil beat Mexico 4-0 with two goals from Ademir. Mexico's goalkeeper, Antonio Carbajal, would go on to set a record, appearing in five separate World Cups.

FIFA had decided to go back to mini-leagues for the first round instead of direct knock-out. Brazil won their group easily. England were widely expected to win group two. Instead, they failed in sensational fashion after losing 1-0 to the United States in Belo Horizonte. The most famous upset in World Cup history was achieved by one goal from the Americans' Haitian centre-forward Larry Gaetjens. England's team included all-time greats such as Billy Wright, Tom Finney and Stan Mortensen.

Defending title-holders Italy also failed in their group, which was won by Sweden. The Italians did have an excuse: 10 senior internationals, the nucleus of their team, had been killed in an air disaster in Turin the previous year.

The final round was also a mini-league. The last game pitted Brazil against old rivals Uruguay. As it happened, Brazil needed only a draw to win the World Cup. A world record crowd of almost 200,000 turned out to celebrate . . . and went home in mourning. Brazil, despite taking an early lead, lost 2-1. Uruguay were World Cup-winners for a second time.

WORLD CUP FINAL

Uruguay 2	Brazil 1
Schaffino, Ghiggia	Friaca

Rio de Janeiro, July 16: 199,854

Uruguay: Maspoli, M Gonzalez, Tejera, Gambetta, Varela, Andrade, Ghiggia, Perez, Miguez, Schiaffino, Moran.

Brazil: Barbosa, Augusto, Juvenal, Bauer, Danilo, Bigode, Friaca, Zizinho, Ademir, Jair, Chico.

Tournament leading scorer:
Ademir de Menezes (Brazil) 9 goals.

The first England squad to compete in the World Cup are about to leave for Brazil. A humiliating defeat by the USA lay ahead.

1954 in SWITZERLAND

Hungary were the clearest World Cup favourites ever. Unbeaten for four years, their rampage through Europe had included historic 6-3 and 7-1 victories over England home and away.

WORLD CUP FINAL

Germany 3	Hungary 2
Morlock, Rahn 2	Puskas, Czibor

Berne, July 4: 60,000

Germany: Turek, Posipal, Kohlmeyer, Eckel, Liebrich, Mai, Rahn, Morlock, O Walter, F Walter, Schafer.

Hungary: Grosics, Buzansky, Lantos, Bozsik, Lorant, Zakarias, Czibor, Kocsis, Hidegkuti, Puskas, M Toth.

Tournament leading scorer:
Sandor Kocsis (Hungary) 11 goals.

Hungary's team had great inside forwards in Sandor Kocsis and skipper Ferenc Puskas and a revolutionary tactical concept with the centre-forward dropping back into midfield.

Again, the format for the finals was changed. This time it was four groups of four nations with the top two entering knock-out quarter-finals.

Brazil and Yugoslavia topped group one, Uruguay and Austria topped group three (Uruguay thrashed Scotland 7-0 on the way) and England and Italy topped group four. Group two, predictably, was headed by Hungary with Germany as runners-up. The Germans had qualified despite deliberately fielding a weakened team against Hungary and being thrashed 8-3.

The quarter-finals ranged from the thriller in which Austria beat hosts Switzerland 7-5 to the bad-tempered Battle of Bern in which Hungary beat Brazil 4-2. Three players were sent off and fighting continued in the dressing rooms after the game.

West Germany easily beat Austria 6-1 in the first semi-final. The other was rated as perhaps the greatest match ever, with Hungary defeating Uruguay 4-2. Kocsis headed two goals in extra time to inflict Uruguay's first World Cup defeat.

Hungary's Final gamble in recalling the half-fit Puskas appeared to pay off when they seized a 2-0 lead inside the first 11 minutes. Then they relaxed – always a fatal mistake against German teams. Two late goals from Helmut Rahn sent Hungary tumbling to defeat in the one match which mattered most.

The traditional exchange of pennants takes place before the final between the great Ferenc Puskas and the West German captain, Walter.

in SWEDEN

The 1958 finals seemed wide-open. Hosts Sweden and holders Germany faced a challenge from France inspired by the scoring talents of Juste Fontaine and the creative skills of Raymond Kopa.

1958

WORLD CUP FINAL

Brazil 5
Vava 2 Pele 2, Zagalo

Sweden 2
Liedholm, Simonsson

Stockholm, June 29: 49,737

Brazil: Gilmar, D Santos, N Santos, Zito, Bellini, Orlando, Garrincha, Didi, Vava, Pele, Zagalo.

Sweden: Svensson, Bergmark, Axbom, Borjesson, Gustavsson, Parling, Hamrin, Gren, Simonsson, Liedholm, Skoglund.

Tournament leading scorer:
Juste Fontaine (France) 13 goals.

But, ultimately, the finals were dominated by Brazil who brought a new tactical scheme in 4-2-4 and some of the greatest individual talents the game has ever seen. Chief among these was a 17-year-old named Pele and a bandy-legged right winger, Garrincha.

Manager Vicente Feola left both of them out of Brazil's first two matches, a 3-0 win over Austria and a goalless draw with England. But his senior players pleaded with Feola to give Pele and Garrincha their chance. The outcome was a 2-0 win over newcomers Soviet Union, which provided the springboard to 12 years of almost uninterrupted World Cup supremacy.

The 1958 finals saw all four British home countries present together for the one and only time. England, their team torn apart by Manchester United's Munich air disaster in the February, fell in the first round. So did Scotland. But Northern Ireland and Wales both reached the quarter-finals where the Irish crashed to France but Wales lost by just Pele's single goal to Brazil.

Pele also grabbed a hat-trick as Brazil thrashed France in the semi-finals while the speed and skill of wingers Hamrin and Skoglund saw hosts Sweden upset holders Germany 3-1. In the Final, however, Sweden were no match for Brazil and Pele wept tears of joy after scoring twice. Brazil's 5-2 win made them the only nation ever to win the World Cup on the 'wrong' continent.

The 17-year old Pele about to wheel away in triumph after scoring Brazil's fourth goal during their 5-2 demolition of Sweden in the Final.

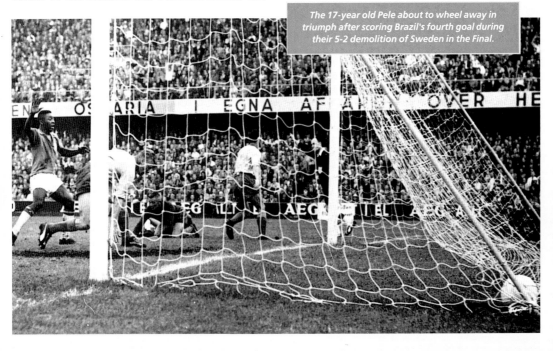

1962 in CHILE

Chile staged the finals despite the ravages of an earthquake. Host nation pride encouraged both the organisers and also the Chilean players who ended third – by far their best World Cup finish.

WORLD CUP FINAL

Brazil 3   **Czechoslovakia 1**
Amarildo,   Masopust
Zito, Vava

Santiago, June 17: 68,679.

Brazil: Gilmar, D Santos, N Santos, Zito, Mauro, Zozimo, Garrincha, Didi, Vava, Amarildo, Zagalo.

Czechoslovakia: Schroiff, Ticjy, Novak, Pluskal, Popluhar, Masopust, Pospichal, Scherer, Kvasniak, Kadrada, Jelinek.

Tournament leading scorers:
Valentin Ivanov (Soviet Union), Leonel Sanchez (Chile), Garrincha, Vava (Brazil), Florian Albert (Hungary), Drazen Jerkovic (Yugoslavia) 4 each.

The format was the now-settled one with four groups of four teams followed by knock-out quarter-finals. The early stages were marred, however, by some bad tempered matches. The worst saw Chile beat Italy 2-0 in one of the most brutal games ever seen in the World Cup. Two Italians were sent off while Chile's Leonel Sanchez was lucky to stay on the field after a punch, unseen by English referee Ken Aston, which broke the nose of Italy's Humberto Maschio.

Brazil made a slow start. Pele scored a wonderful goal in their opening 2-0 win over Mexico but was then injured and missed the rest of the finals.

However, Brazil found, in Amarildo, a brilliant deputy. He scored twice as Brazil recovered from 1-0 down to beat Spain 2-1 in their decisive group match.

Three fancied European nations, the Soviet Union, Germany and England, all fell in the quarter-finals. But results guaranteed a Europe v South America Final. In the all-European semi Czechoslovakia, inspired by mid-fielder Josef Masopust, beat Yugoslavia 3-1 while the all-South American tie saw Brazil defeat Chile 4-2. Two-goal hero Garrincha was sent off for kicking Chile's Eladio Rojas but, to Brazil's relief, not suspended.

Czechoslovakia, making their second appearance in the Final, led through Masopust but Brazil hit back when Amarildo squeezed a shot between goalkeeper Schroiff and his near post. That was enough encouragement and Brazil went on to win their second successive World Cup.

Having come in as a replacement for the injured Pele, Amarildo is embraced by Brazilian supporters after scoring both his side's goals in the 2-1 defeat of Spain.

in ENGLAND

England's greatest day in football history earned a knighthood for the manager Alf Ramsey and places in legend for team skipper Bobby Moore, midfield maestro Bobby Charlton and striker Geoff Hurst.

19

Yet England found goal-scoring tough in the first round, being held goalless in the opening match by Uruguay and beating Mexico and France 'only' 2-0 apiece. No such problems for West Germany. A brilliant youngster named Franz Beckenbauer inspired a five-goal show first time out against Switzerland.

Brazil struggled. The double World Cup-winners mistakenly brought back too many of their veteran winners from 1958 and 1962 and failed to survive the first-round group matches after Pele was kicked out of the tournament by stop-at-nothing defenders from Bulgaria and Portugal.

The greatest shock of the opening rounds was staged in Middlesbrough where North Korea – the mysterious unknowns of the event – defeated the highly-paid professionals of Italy by 1-0. A goal from Pak Do Ik sent Italy home to the rotten tomato treatment.

The North Koreans very nearly went on to repeat the shock in the quarter-finals. They led Portugal 3-0 before being beaten 5-3 on the day which also saw Argentina threaten to walk out of the World Cup after the expulsion of skipper Antonio Rattin in a 1-0 defeat by England.

By contrast, England's semi-final game against Portugal was one of the most sporting ever seen. Bobby Charlton scored twice for England to set up the dramatic Final in which West Germany were beaten 4-2 with Geoff Hurst scoring the only ever World Cup final hat-trick – though the Germans complained that Hurst's second goal bounced back into play rather than across the goal-line, as the referee, Mr Dienst, decided.

WORLD CUP FINAL

England 4	West Germany 2
Hurst 3, Peters	Haller, Weber
After extra time	

Wembley, July 30: 96,924

England: Banks, Cohen, Wilson, Stiles, J.Charlton, Moore, Ball, Hunt, B Charlton, Hurst, Peters.

West Germany: Tilkowski, Hottges, Schnellinger, Beckenbauer, Schulz, Weber, Haller, Overath, Seeler, Held, Emmerich.

Tournament leading scorer: Eusebio da Silva (Portugal) 9 goals.

Left back Ray Wilson, flanked by the Charlton brothers, Bobby and Jackie, crowns himself with the trophy during England's lap of honour after the 4-2 defeat of West Germany.

1970

in MEXICO

In Mexico, many matches were played at altitude in the midday heat and humidity to suit European TV. The players hated it but it meant slower, more skilful football and some superb entertainment.

WORLD CUP FINAL

Brazil 4	Italy 1
Pele, Jairzinho, Gerson, Carlos Alberto	Boninsegna

Mexico City, June 21: 107,000

Brazil: Felix, Carlos Alberto, Brito, Wilson Piazza, Everaldo, Clodoaldo, Gerson, Rivelino, Jairzinho, Tostao, Pele.

Italy: Albertosi, Burgnich, Cera, Rosato, Facchetti, Bertini (Juliano), Domenghini, De Sisti, Mazzola, Boninsegna (Rivera), Riva.

Tournament leading scorer: Gerd Muller (West Germany) 10 goals.

Brazil and England, the two most favoured nations, were both unluckily drawn in the same first-round group. Brazil won a titanic match 1-0 with a goal from Jairzinho – who went on to make World Cup history by scoring in every round in the finals.

This was perhaps Brazil's finest team of them all. Pele was fully fit again and at his inspirational best. Against Czechoslovakia in the first round he very nearly scored with a long shot from inside his own half after spotting the Czechoslovak goalkeeper way off his line. In Brazil's semi-final victory over Uruguay, Pele pulled off a wonderful 'wrong-way' dummy around the Uruguayan goalkeeper.

England's World Cup defence ended in the quarter-finals. Goalkeeper Gordon Banks was taken ill on the eve of the match against old rivals West Germany in Leon. This did not appear a problem when England surged into a two-goal lead. But deputy Peter Bonetti's lack of match practice in the conditions proved significant when Germany fought back to win 3-2 in extra-time with goals from Beckenbauer, veteran skipper Uwe Seeler and tournament top scorer Gerd Muller.

The efforts West Germany put in to win that game counted against them in a wonderful semi-final against Italy. Again the Germans took the match into extra time but this time it was the Italians who triumphed, by 4-3, to reach the Final.

In the Final, as waves of Brazilian attacks came in to the background beat of a samba rhythm, Italy were showing clear signs of fatigue and were eventually overrun as Brazil achieved the first World Cup hat-trick.

Brazilian right-back and captain, Carlos Alberto, takes the field alongside Italy's Facchetti just before the start of the great 1970 Final.

in WEST GERMANY

1974

Holland's exciting 'total football' thrilled the TV millions who tuned in to the 1974 finals. But in the end their West German hosts proved that application matters as much as skill and entertainment.

These two nations brought to the finals the world game's two outstanding individuals now that Pele had retired from the international scene: Johan Cruyff, the Flying Dutchman, and Franz Beckenbauer, Kaiser Franz, so nicknamed both for his personal command and his arrogant technique.

It took the Germans, as usual, half the tournament to get into their stride. But not Holland. Cruyff justified the £922,000 world record fee Barcelona had paid Ajax Amsterdam in his first game when he glided over a string of ferocious Uruguayan tackles to inspire a 2-0 victory. Later came equally impressive victories over Bulgaria, Argentina, East Germany and outgoing champions Brazil to earn a place in the Final in Munich.

Beckenbauer and Co had more difficulty. They even lost 1-0 to their cousins and neighbours from East Germany in the nations' first and only meeting before squeezing into the second round.

Unfortunately for Holland, the Germans had timed it just right. Holland took a rapid-fire lead in the Final when English referee Jack Taylor awarded the first-ever penalty in a World Cup final. Johan Neeskens converted it so Holland led 1-0 before any of the German players had yet touched the ball. But the Dutch grew so intent on looking good that they lost sight of the need to score more goals.

That was a mistake Beckenbauer and Co did not make. Paul Breitner equalised from another penalty and, shortly before half-time, marksman supreme Gerd Muller scored the decisive goal.

WORLD CUP FINAL

West Germany 2	Holland 1
Breitner penalty, Muller	Neeskens penalty

Munich, July 7: 77,833

West Germany: Maier, Vogts, Schwarzenbeck, Beckenbauer, Breitner, Bonhof, Honess, Overath, Grabowski, Muller, Holzenbein

Holland: Jongbloed, Suurbier, Rijsbergen (De Jong), Haan, Krol, Jansen, Van Hanegem, Neeskens, Rep, Cruyff, Rensenbrink (R Van der Kerkhof).

Tournament leading scorer: Grzegorz Lato (Poland) 7 goals.

Two of the linchpins of the great 1970s West German sides, goal poacher Gerd Muller (left) and attacking full-back Paul Breitner (right).

1978 in ARGENTINA

The football world wondered just what they would find when the four-yearly global circus arrived in Argentina two years after a military coup. They found a country which had gone football-mad.

WORLD CUP FINAL

Argentina 3	Holland 1
Kempes 2, Bertoni	Nanninga

Buenos Aires, June 25: 77,260

Argentina: Fillol, Olguin, Galvan, Passarella, Tarantini, Ardiles (Larrosa), Gallego, Kempes, Bertoni, Luque, Ortiz (Houseman).

Holland: Jongbloed, Jansen (Suurbier), Brandts, Krol, Poortvliet, W Van der Kerkhof, Neeskens, Haan, R Van der Kerkhof, Rep (Nanninga), Rensenbrink.

Tournament leading scorer:
Mario Kempes (Argentina) six goals.

Argentina had, for years, been the world's greatest exporter of footballers. Now they had a manager in Cesar Luis Menotti who, with the federation's backing, had briefly been given the power to veto transfers abroad and recall the one player who made all the difference – Mario Kempes, from Spanish club Valencia.

Italy, the best of the European challengers, did manage to beat Argentina in a first-round group match. Italy had discovered a quick-silver centre-forward named Paolo Rossi whose partnership up front with big Roberto Bettega took Italy through to fourth place. But they were pushed out of a place in the Final by the power-shooting of Holland's Arie Haan and Ernie Brandts in their decisive second-round tie.

Argentina met Holland in the Final after some rapid-fire finishing of their own in the second round. Argentina came to their last match, against Peru, needing to win by four clear goals to edge ahead of Brazil on goal difference. Peru hit a post in only the second minute but that was the last anyone saw of their attack. After that it was all Argentina, who duly won 6-0 to reach 'their' Final.

Holland were without Johan Cruyff. He had retired from the national team after the qualifying matches. Yet Holland so nearly won. At 1-1 Ron Rensenbrink shot against a post with just minutes remaining. But Argentina proved the stronger in extra time and ran out 3-1 winners amid ticker-tape celebrations.

Mario Kempes, the player of the tournament and scorer of two goals in the Final, takes the ball past the talented and powerful Dutch midfielder Rudi Krol.

in SPAIN

Italy took a huge gamble in including centre-forward Paolo Rossi because the Juventus spearhead had only played the final three games of the league season after a two-year ban.

19

The gamble appeared misplaced when Italy only scraped through their first round group after being held to draws, not only by Poland, but by the dangerously unpredictable African qualifiers from Cameroon.

But, once into the second round, both Italy and Rossi found their shooting boots. Tardelli and Cabrini scored the goals which effectively eliminated holders Argentina and Rossi snatched an opportunist hat-trick to secure a brilliant 3-2 win over Brazil. Rossi then scored both goals in a comparatively simple victory over Poland and Italy were into the Final for the fourth time in their history.

Their West German opponents found progress even more awkward. They lost to Algeria, a major shock, then squeezed through only thanks to a disgraceful, mutually convenient 1-0 victory over Austria.

The number of nations taking part in the finals was increased this year from 16 to 24. For the first time since 1962 a goal was scored in the Opening Match – and it was against holders Argentina who lost 1-0 to Belgium.

Other nations were to make bigger headlines, such as Northern Ireland with their surprise win over uninspired hosts Spain in the first round and Kuwait for a collective walk-out in the middle of a defeat by France. England, back in the finals for the first time since 1970, reached the second round but were undermined by injuries to key players Kevin Keegan and Trevor Brooking.

West Germany reached the Final after a most dramatic victory on penalties over France in the semi-final in Seville. But their luck ran out there. Italy, despite seeing Cabrini miss a penalty of their own, still beat the Germans 3-1 in the Final.

WORLD CUP FINAL

Italy 3	West Germany 1
Rossi, Tardelli, Altobelli	Breitner

Madrid, July 11; 90,000

Italy: Zoff, Bergomi, Collovati, Scirea, Gentile, Cabrini, Tardelli, Oriali, Conti, Rossi, Graziani (Altobelli; Causio).

West Germany: Schumacher, Kaltz, K.Forster, B Forster, Stielike, Briegel, Dremmler (Hrubesch), Breitner, Rummenigge (H Muller), Fischer, Littbarski.

Tournament leading scorer: Paolo Rossi (Italy) 6 goals.

Paolo Rossi, the tournament's leading scorer in 1982, turns in triumph after completing his hat-trick against Brazil in Italy's second round 3-2 victory.

1986 in MEXICO

Diego Maradona dominated the 1986 World Cup finals in Mexico. Argentina's captain and inspiration was unchallenged as the greatest natural talent to emerge in the world game since Pele.

WORLD CUP FINAL

Argentina 3   **West Germany 2**
Brown, Valdano,   Rummenigge, Voller
Burruchaga

Mexico City, June 29: 114,590

Argentina: Pumpido, Cuciuffo, Brown, Ruggeri, Giusti, Burruchaga (Trobbiani), Batista, Enrique, Olarticoechea, Maradona, Valdano.

West Germany: Schumacher, Berthold, Jakobs, K Forster, Briegel, Brehme, Matthaus, Magath (D Hoeness), Eder, Rummenigge, K Allofs (Voller).

Tournament leading scorer:
Gary Lineker (England) 6 goals.

But controversy followed him everywhere and Mexico'86 was no exception. As for the host nation, Mexico delighted their fans by reaching the quarter-finals, where they lost only on penalties to a West German side managed by former Cup-winning captain Franz Beckenbauer. In an all-European semi-final, West Germany then beat France 2-0, repeating their success at the same stage in 1982.

France, led by the great Michel Platini, had previously won the finals' outstanding game when they defeated Brazil on penalties in the quarter-finals. Brazil's superstar Zico missed a second-half spot-kick and skipper Socrates was crucially off target in the shoot-out.

Argentina's path to the Final had been comfortable up until their quarter-final meeting with England. Bobby Robson's men had hit form with an impressive 3-0 victory in their last group match against Poland thanks to a Gary Lineker hat-trick. Lineker went on to finish as the tournament's top scorer with six goals.

The quarter-final between England and Argentina was surrounded by security fears because of the Falklands War four years earlier. But the real controversy was out on the pitch after the Tunisian referee awarded Argentina an opening goal even though Maradona had clearly punched a chip forward beyond goalkeeper Peter Shilton. England's protests were in vain and min-

utes later Maradona embarked on a solo slalom from inside his own half to score – by comparison – one of the finest individual goals ever seen in the World Cup finals.

Clearly, Argentina's name was on the Cup – as they confirmed by defeating West Germany 3-2 in the Final. The Germans hit back from 2-0 down to level 2-2 at one stage. But this was one occasion on which their talent for recovery proved in vain and Maradona carried off the World Cup.

Diego Maradona clutches the trophy after Argentina had defeated West Germany 3-2 before 115,000 people at the Aztec Stadium.

in ITALY

1990

ENGLAND, under Bobby Robson once more, enjoyed their finest World Cup since 1966. They had been tucked away on the island of Sardinia for their opening group, a decision based on security advice.

But it was not until England reached the Italian mainland after the group matches had been completed that their campaign came to life.

In the second round David Platt's late, late goal in extra time from a Paul Gascoigne free-kick defeated Belgium. Then two superbly-struck penalties by Gary Lineker saw England edge past African surprises, Cameroon, by 3-2 in the quarter-finals.

The semi-final against West Germany in Turin was a dramatic classic. West Germany went ahead through a deflected free-kick from Andy Brehme on

the hour but Lineker's 80th-minute equaliser earned extra time. No more goals were scored so the tie went to penalties and failures by Stuart Pearce and Chris Waddle allowed West Germany to head for the Final in Rome.

Their opponents, once more, were Argentina. Not the skilled, outgoing Argentina of 1986 but a much more negative outfit who relied on the penalty-stopping talents

of goalkeeper Sergio Goycochea to overcome Yugoslavia in the quarter-finals and hosts Italy in the semi-finals. Ironically it was an orthodox penalty, converted after 80 minutes of the Final in Rome by Andy Brehme, which decided the World Cup in West Germany's favour.

German skipper Lothar Matthaus was voted Player

of the Finals while explosive new Italian striker Toto Schillaci was six-goal tournament top scorer. Surprise packet were Cameroon, who beat Argentina 1-0 in the opening match in Milan despite having two players sent off.

WORLD CUP FINAL

West Germany 1   **Argentina 0**
Brehme penalty

Rome, July 8: 73,603.

West Germany: Illgner, Berthold (Reuter), Kohler, Augenthaler, Buchwald, Brehme, Hassler, Matthaus, Littbarski, Voller, Klinsmann.

Argentina: Goycochea, Lorenzo, Sensini, Serrizuela, Ruggeri (Monzon), Simon, Jose Horacio Basualdo, Burruchaga (Calderon), Maradona, Troglio, Dezotti.

Tournament leading scorer:
Salvatore Schillaci (Italy) 6 goals.

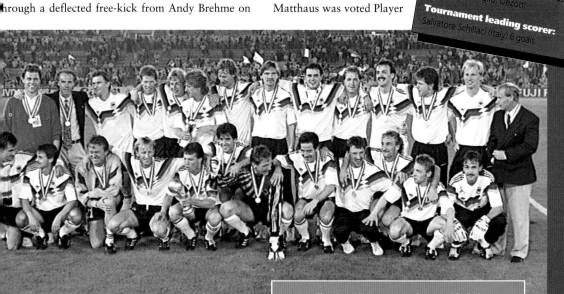

The West German squad pose with their Cup-winners' medals after defeating Argentina in a disappointing end to the 1990 tournament which was decided on a late penalty.

World Cup '94

World Cup Hall of Fame

ANTONIO CARBAJAL
Mexico

Only one man has appeared in no fewer than five World Cup finals tournaments and he is the legendary Mexican goalkeeper who appeared in 1950, 1954, 1958, 1962 and in England in 1966. Later Carbajal was honoured with FIFA's Gold Medal in recognition of his World Cup feat and his outstanding sportsmanship.

FRANZ BECKENBAUER
West Germany

'Kaiser Franz' made history as the only man to win the World Cup as both captain (in 1974) and then manager (in 1990). Beckenbauer made his finals debut in 1966 in midfield but later, with Bayern Munich, moved back to revolutionise the role of sweeper. His total of 103 caps was for years a German record.

JOHN CHARLES
Wales

Wales have reached the finals only once, when Charles was their mainstay - either at centre-half or centre-forward - in 1958. Charles, nicknamed the Gentle Giant, made his name with Leeds before transferring to Italy's Juventus for a then British record £67,000 in 1957.

GIANPIERO COMBI
Italy

Combi is still considered by many veteran experts as having been Italy's greatest goalkeeper. He starred throughout the 1930s for Juventus, helping them win five league titles in a row, and was captain of the Italian side who won the 1934 World Cup. Combi played 47 times for his country.

JOHAN CRUYFF
Holland

Three times Cruyff was voted European Footballer of the Year thanks to his club success at centre-forward for Ajax Amsterdam and then Barcelona. He captained and inspired Holland to reach the 1974 World Cup Final. Now, back with Barcelona, he ranks among the world's most successful coaches.

BOBBY CHARLTON
England

A Munich air crash survivor in 1958, Charlton was one of the original Busby Babes and the epitome of the great English sportsman. His vital goals against Mexico and Portugal helped inspire England's World Cup triumph in 1966 which Bobby celebrated with centre-half brother Jack.

20

DIDI Brazil

Waldir Pereira (Didi's real name) played in the 1954 finals, then starred as Brazil's World Cup-winning midfield general in 1958 and 1962. He played most of his club career in Rio de Janeiro with Botafogo, moving to Europe only briefly in 1959 with Real Madrid. His speciality was the 'falling leaf' free kick.

KENNY DALGLISH
Scotland

Scotland have had a mixed time of it at the World Cup finals but Dalglish's value to his country was never in doubt and he later became the first Scotland player to top a century of caps. Dalglish, who began with Celtic, joined Liverpool in 1977 and later managed them to the league-and-cup double.

JUSTE FONTAINE
France

In Sweden in 1958, Fontaine set a record of 13 goals in one finals tournament which may never be beaten. Yet he owed his place in the French team only to an injury to Rene Bliard. Sadly, Fontaine's own career was cut short by leg injuries. Moroccan-born, he played his club football with Reims.

EUSEBIO Portugal

Eusebio da Silva Ferreira counts among the World Cup heroes although he played in only one finals tournament. That was enough to secure legend status after he top-scored with nine goals, including the late penalty against the Soviet Union which sealed Portugal's best-ever third-place finish.

GERSON
Brazil

Brazil have a tradition of producing great midfield generals. Gerson succeeded Didi as creative commander not only of Brazil but of Rio de Janeiro's Botafogo club. His long-range shooting scared goalkeepers and Gerson plundered a typical goal against Italy in the 1970 World Cup Final.

GARRINCHA
Brazil

Manoel Francisco dos Santos was perhaps the greatest right wing of all time, despite childhood illness which left his legs painfully twisted. Garrincha (his nickname meant Little Bird) only got into Brazil's team in 1958 after a team-mates' deputation pressed his case with manager Vicente Feola.

GEOFF HURST
England

Hurst remains the only man to have scored a hat-trick in a World Cup Final. Originally a wing-half, he was converted into one of the outstanding strikers in the world by West Ham manager Ron Greenwood and stepped into England's 1966 World Cup side after injury ruled out Jimmy Greaves.

ALCIDES GHIGGIA Uruguay

Ghiggia was nicknamed the 'Suicide Winger' after his goal, in the Maracana, condemned Brazil to defeat in the 1950 World Cup Final. He made his name with Montevideo giants Penarol, then transferred in 1953 to Italy where he played eight seasons with Roma before winding down his career with MIlan.

JAIRZINHO
Brazil

Jairzinho exploded in the late 1960s in the tradition of great Brazilian right-wingers such as Julinho and Garrincha. Like Garrincha he played for Botafogo of Rio. Unlike anyone else in football history, he scored a goal in every round in the finals in 1970 in Mexico.

SANDOR KOCSIS
Hungary

Kocsis was nicknamed the 'Man with the Golden Head' because of his brilliance in the air. He was inside forward partner to Ferenc Puskas in the Hungarian team of the early 1950s and later played with huge success for Barcelona. Kocsis was 11-goal top scorer – then a record haul – at the 1954 World Cup.

MARIO KEMPES Argentina

Cesar Menotti, Argentina's 1978 World Cup boss, fetched home only one exiled star for the finals. Kempes, who played in Spain with Valencia, added vital extra Cup-winning punch to Argentina's attack. His six goals included two in Argentina's 3-1 victory over Holland in the Final.

GARY LINEKER
England

In Mexico in 1986 Lineker became the only British player ever to top-score at the World Cup. His six goals included a first-round hat-trick against Poland at the peak of a worldwide career which took him from Leicester and Everton to Barcelona back to Tottenham and onto Japan with Grampus Eight.

GRZEGORZ LATO
Poland

Poland's superb team in the 1970s owed as much to the sharp-shooting of Lato as to the creative talents of Kaziu Deyna and Robert Gadocha. Lato ended his career in Mexico after top-scoring with seven goals at the 1974 World Cup and adding another two in 1978. Lato played 103 times for Poland.

JOSEF MASOPUST
Czechoslovakia

Masopust, a tireless worker in midfield from an old-fashioned nominal left-half position, became the only Czechoslovak ever to be honoured as European Footballer of the Year for his exploits at the 1962 finals. Masopust even opened the scoring in the Final before the Czechs went down 3-1 to Brazil.

LEONIDAS DA SILVA
Brazil

Leonidas was Brazil's first World Cup superstar in the 1930s. He was the first centre-forward to perfect the overhead bicycle kick and reached his peak in the 1938 finals when he scored four goals in a sensational 6-5 win over Poland. Leonidas's career brought him 25 goals in 24 internationals.

World Cup Hall of Fame

GIUSEPPE MEAZZA
Italy

Meazza was a great goal-scoring inside forward with Italy, Milan and Internazionale in the 1930s. He was also one of the only two players to survive from Italy's 1934 World Cup-winning side through to victory again in 1938 (the other was Giovanni Ferrari, Meazza's inside-forward partner).

BOBBY MOORE
England

Wembley was a second home to Bobby Moore. With West Ham he won the FA Cup there in 1964 and the European Cup-winners' Cup in 1965; in 1966 he carried off the World Cup with England. In doing so, Moore also earned accolades as one of the greatest central defenders of all time.

ROGER MILLA
Cameroon

Veteran Milla was Cameroon's goal-grabbing 'super-sub' at the 1990 finals. A former African Footballer of the Year, he celebrated his goals by dancing round the corner flags – never with more delight than after the goal which beat Colombia and sent Cameroon into the 1990 quarter-finals.

GERD MULLER West Germany

Despite his lack of height, Muller was one of the most phenomenal marksmen in history, scoring 68 goals in 62 internationals - including a total of 14 in the finals of 1970 and 1974 and the winning goal against Holland in the Final of 1974 in Munich, his home stadium in the club game with Bayern.

JOSE NASAZZI Uruguay

Nasazzi entered history as the first captain to hold aloft the World Cup trophy after Uruguay's home-town victory in 1930. He was also one of the greatest right-backs of the pre-war era, playing 64 times for Uruguay and winning Olympic gold in both 1924 and 1928.

DANIEL PASSARELLA
Argentina

Every top team needs an influential captain and Passarella was just that for Argentina in 1978. Rugged and powerful, he brought the ball out of defence time and again to set his midfield to work. Passarella later played with great success in Italy before returning home to coach his old club, River Plate.

OLDRICH NEJEDLY
Czechoslovakia

Nejedly was a star inside-left not only with runners-up Czechoslovakia at the 1934 World Cup but for Sparta Prague, one of Europe's greatest clubs in the 1930s. The Czechs' 1938 World Cup bid ended when Nejedly broke a leg in a rugged quarter-final against Brazil.

World Cup '94

PELE Brazil

Edson Arantes do Nascimento was the greatest player in World Cup history. In 1958, at 17, he hit two goals in Brazil's 5-2 defeat of Sweden and he scored in the 1970 victory over Italy. In between, injuries reduced Pele's contribution to Brazil's 1962 win while ruthless defenders were scandalously allowed to kick him out of the 1966 finals in England.

MICHEL PLATINI
France

French football knew the greatest decade in its history in the 1980s thanks to the brilliance of skipper and attacking midfielder Michel Platini. He top-scored and captained the team which won the 1984 European Championship and led France to the semi-finals of both the 1982 and 1986 World Cups.

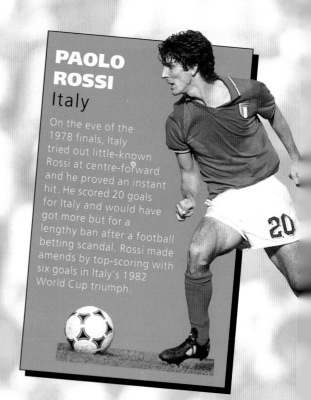

FERENC PUSKAS
Hungary

Puskas was inside left and captain of the magical Hungarian team of the early 1950s and later starred for Real Madrid. Puskas relied only on his left foot but that was more than enough to lead Hungary to their legendary 6-3 win over England at Wembley and to a fabulous run of four years unbeaten.

PAOLO ROSSI
Italy

On the eve of the 1978 finals, Italy tried out little-known Rossi at centre-forward and he proved an instant hit. He scored 20 goals for Italy and would have got more but for a lengthy ban after a football betting scandal. Rossi made amends by top-scoring with six goals in Italy's 1982 World Cup triumph.

LUIGI RIVA   Italy

A resilient left-winger turned central striker, Riva battled back twice from broken legs to become one of the most prolific marksmen in Italian history in the late 1960s and early 1970s, scoring 35 goals in 42 internationals in one of the most defensive eras in the game's history.

GIANNI RIVERA
Italy

At 15, a half-share in Rivera cost Milan £90,000 and he was nicknamed Italy's 'Golden Boy'. He was a stylish, creative inside-forward. In 1970, even though often used only for half a game, he was instrumental in steering Italy back to the World Cup Final for the first time in more than 30 years.

GYORGY SAROSI
Hungary

Sarosi was the greatest Hungarian footballer before Puskas. He starred in the 1930s either at centre-forward or centre-half. A qualified doctor, he still found time to lead Hungary to runners-up spot at the 1938 World Cup finals. Sarosi was three times top scorer in Hungary before moving to Italy with Genoa.

SALVATORE SCHILLACI
Italy

In 1989 Juventus bought Sicilian centre-forward 'Toto' Schillaci almost as an afterthought. But a year later they possessed the hottest property in the Italian game after he exploded as six-goal top scorer to lead his country, as host nation, to third place in the World Cup finals.

UWE SEELER
West Germany

German fans used Seeler's name – 'Uwe, Uwe' – as a chant to support their team for 16 years between 1954, when he made his debut at 17, until his retirement after the 1970 World Cup. He was a brave and robust centre-forward whose loyalty to Hamburg - his only club - was appreciated by the fans.

OBDULIO VARELA
Uruguay

More than any other player, Uruguayan captain Varela was responsible for Uruguay's shock 1950 World Cup triumph over Brazil. An attacking centre-half of the old school, he drove his men forward with limitless energy and self-confidence to triumph over all the odds in the Maracana.

GUILLERMO STABILE   Argentina

Stabile was Argentina's first World Cup superstar, top-scoring with eight goals from centre-forward for the side who finished runners-up in the inaugural World Cup. He began with Independiente of Buenos Aires and later played in Italy with Genoa and in Spain with Real Madrid.

LEV YASHIN   Soviet Union

Yashin was just about to give up soccer and switch to ice hockey instead when he was given his chance with Moscow Dynamo. He went on to win Olympic gold in 1956 and bring his legendary agility and sportsmanship to the World Cups of 1958, 1962 and 1966 – when the Soviets finished a best-ever fourth.

ZICO   Brazil

Artur Antunes Coimbra scored with a typical bending Brazilian free kick on his international debut against Uruguay as a teenager. He was nicknamed the 'White Pele', because he succeeded the old hero's No 10 shirt and, despite injuries, was one of the superstars of the 1978, 1982 and 1986 World Cups.

DINO ZOFF
Italy

Zoff became the oldest World Cup-winner when he captained Italy, as goalkeeper, to their triumph in Spain in 1982. He played an Italian record 112 internationals between 1968 and 1983 and once went 1,200 minutes of senior national team football without conceding a goal.

GERMANY

Winners: 1954, 1974, 1990

Germany are grateful to have been spared the nervous rigours of having to qualify for the finals.

THE MANAGER

BERTI VOGTS

Born December 30, 1946
96 international appearances
Appointed July 1990

Ever since the 1-0 victory over Argentina in Rome in 1990 they have been certain of lining up at the Opening Match in Chicago.

But that does not mean manager Berti Vogts has had a quiet life. Quite the opposite. Vogts, who stepped up to succeed Franz Beckenbauer after the Germans completed their World Cup hat-trick, has been under intense pressure from media and fans. He has been criticised for selecting the wrong players or using the right players but the wrong tactics. He has been criticised for sticking with veterans such as Lothar Matthaus and Guido Buchwald and for experimenting with youngsters such as Christian Ziege.

But then, the Germans are proud of their World Cup heritage. Winners in 1954, they were fourth in 1958, quarter-finalists in 1962, runners-up in 1966, third in 1970, winners in 1974 and runners-up again in 1982 and 1986 before triumphing in Rome thanks to a late penalty from leftback Andy Brehme – who was even recalled to the colours last autumn for a 2-1 victory over Brazil in a friendly.

Rudi Voller has retired from the national team so his attacking mantle now falls fully on lanky Jurgen Klinsmann, who now plays his club football in France with Monaco after three successful seasons in Italy with Internazionale.

It is to one of the exiles who remains in Italy that all Germany looks to inspire the World Cup defence. He is Andy Moller, a one-time protege of Vogts in the German youth team a decade ago. Moller was on the substitutes' bench in 1990 but Vogts predicted even then: 'He will be our midfield general in the United States.'

Moller, who has at last put behind him a transfer wrangle involving German clubs Borussia Dortmund and Eintracht Frankfurt, established himself so successfully with Juventus that last year the Turin giants considered England's David Platt had become surplus to requirements.

• Germany's Helmer tackles Brazil's Edmundo.

Then Moller confirmed his international 'arrival' as the match-winning hero of Germany's victory over Brazil last autumn. Practice, perhaps, for the real thing.

- **Left: Stefan Effenberg rides the tackle of Brazil's Paulo Sergios.**

- **Above: Pierre Littbarski and team-mates after the 1990 win.**

- **Right: Jurgen Klinsmann holds off Dave McPherson of Scotland.**

- **Below left: Guido Buchwald, the veteran defender.**

- **Below right: Christian Ziege, Gemany's new full-back.**

ARGENTINA

Winners: 1978, 1986

The mercurial temperament of the Argentinians makes them the Jekyll and Hyde of World Cup football.

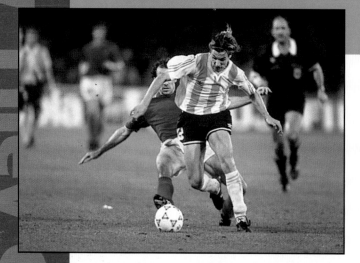

S.AMERICA GROUP A FINAL TABLE

	P	W	D	L	F	A	PTS
COLOMBIA	6	4	2	0	13	2	10
ARGENTINA	6	3	1	2	9	7	7
PARAGUAY	6	1	4	1	6	7	6
PERU	6	0	1	5	4	12	1

Play-off:
1-1, 1-0 v Australia (2-1 agg)

Their players can turn on the most remarkable football skills or descend to the worst excesses of bad temper and bad tackling. That volatile temperament means Argentina can never be discounted as World Cup contenders. Sometimes, as on home ground in 1978 and again in Mexico in 1986, they get the mixture right. Other times, as in Italy four years ago, they get it wrong.

But even when their backs are to the wall Argentina are dangerous. At Italia'90 they beat Yugoslavia in the quarter-finals and hosts Italy in the semi-finals on penalties. In the recent qualifying competition they bounced back from a 5-0 thrashing at home to Colombia to regain their ticket to the United States with a play-off victory over Australia.

The big question to be answered concerns Diego Maradona. Will he play or won't he? Maradona returned to duty against Australia but, after three years away from the international game because of suspension and the sulks, he looked ill at ease. Maradona, who returned home to play for Newell's Old Boys of Rosario, says he is not certain about whether he can withstand the physical and mental pressure of a return to the World Cup finals. But

national boss Alfio Basile is desperate for Maradona's inspirational presence. Also, Basile hopes to revive Maradona's attacking partnership with flying winger Claudio Caniggia, who will be available again after suspension for failing a dope test while playing in Italy.

Sergio Goycochea remains perhaps the world's top goalkeeper and certainly the top penalty-stopper; Fernando Redondo, from Spain's Tenerife, is a class act in midfield; and Gabriel Batistuta, from Italy's Fiorentina, provides all the strength and power of an old-fashioned centre-forward.

With or without Maradona, Argentina will take some stopping.

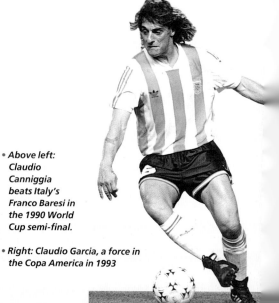

• *Above left: Claudio Canniggia beats Italy's Franco Baresi in the 1990 World Cup semi-final.*

• *Right: Claudio Garcia, a force in the Copa America in 1993*

• Marc de Grijse in action during the match with Wales in Cardiff in 1993.

BELGIUM

Many fans and officials were surprised when Belgium were named among the six top seeds for the World Cup finals.

• Above: Belgium in 1993. Left to right, back: Albert, Van der Elst, Grun, Staelens, Preud'homme, Smidts. Front: Medved, Czerniatynski, Boffin, De Grijse, Scifo.

EUROPEAN GROUP 4 FINAL TABLE							
	P	W	D	L	F	A	Pts
Romania	10	7	1	2	29	12	15
Belgium	10	7	1	2	16	5	15
Czechoslovakia	10	4	5	1	21	9	13
Wales	10	5	2	3	19	12	12
Cyprus	10	2	1	7	8	18	5
Faroe Islands	10	0	0	10	1	38	0

The Belgians owed that honour to two factors – one was England's qualifying failure (since England would have ranked above them), the second was the Belgians' own consistent efforts at the pinnacle of the world game.

The seedings – apart from those of hosts and holders – were computed from nations' records at the last three World Cups. Belgium were second round material in Spain in 1982, semi-finalists (and placed fourth) in Mexico in 1986, then second rounders again in Italy four years ago. It's a proud record on consistency on which manager Paul Van Himst and his players intend to build.

Belgium had, at one stage, threatened to be the first European nation – after the seeded Germans – to secure a place in the finals. They won their first six qualifying matches and went to Wales in March last year needing only one point for security. They lost, instead, by 2-0 and a further defeat by Romania meant it was not until the last moment and the last match, against Czechoslovakia, that Belgium made it.

The players who faltered so unpredictably include some of the most experienced in Europe. Goalkeeper Michel Preud'homme has been a star for a decade while versatile defender Georges Grun was first a mainstay of Anderlecht and then a key factor in the rise of Italian club Parma. Enzo Scifo is one of the most delicately-talented midfielders in Europe and Luc Nilis and Brazilian-born Luis Oliveira experienced strikers.

Belgium may also have a new recruit by the time the finals start. Exiled Croat Josip Weber, long a force in the Belgian league, has just obtained Belgian citizenship and will be clear to play for his adopted homeland ... just in time.

BELGIUM'S RESULTS EUROPEAN GROUP 4
1-0 v Cyprus
3-0 v Faroe Islands
2-1 v Czechoslovakia
1-0 v Romania
2-0 v Wales
0-2 v Wales
3-0 v Faroe Islands
1-2 v Romania
0-0 v Czechoslovakia

THE MANAGER

PAUL VAN HIMST

Born October 2, 1943
81 international appearances
Appointed 1991

29

BOLIVIA

Bolivia last reached the finals in 1950 when they crashed 8-0 to Uruguay and went home after one match.

S. AMERICA GROUP B FINAL TABLE	P	W	D	L	F	A	Pts
Brazil	8	5	2	1	20	4	12
Bolivia	8	5	1	2	22	10	11
Uruguay	8	4	2	2	9	7	10
Ecuador	8	1	3	4	7	7	5
Venezuela	8	1	0	7	4	34	2

**BOLIVIA'S RESULTS
S. AMERICA GROUP B**
7-1 v Venezuela
2-0 v Brazil
3-0 v Uruguay
1-0 v Ecuador
7-0 v Venezuela
0-6 v Brazil
1-2 v Uruguay
1-1 v Ecuador

But in more than 40 years everything has changed. That is the promise and the warning issued by manager Xavier Azkargorta and his team of ambitious unknowns.

Bolivia's arrival in the list of finalists surprised most foreigners. But it didn't surprise the rest of South America. The writing was on the wall when they managed to beat mighty Brazil at the start of their qualifying campaign.

Soccer was introduced to Bolivia in the 1890s and the top club, appropriately named The Strongest, were founded in La Paz in 1908. Bolivia took part in the inaugural World Cup in Uruguay, losing 4-0 to both Yugoslavia and Brazil. Their only subsequent appearance in the finals was their unfortunate one-match excursion to Brazil in 1950. Thus now they anticipate, at the least, scoring their first goal at the World Cup finals.

When they were drawn in a qualifying group which included Brazil and Uruguay no-one gave them a chance. But playing all their home matches at altitude in La Paz and appointing Spaniard Xavier Azkargorta as manager worked a miracle.

His first sight of his players was at the South American championship in Ecuador. Bolivia fell in the first round but Azkargorta recog-

nised their potential. A couple of minor adjustments and Bolivia opened their World Cup campaign with a 7-1 thrashing of Venezuela. Top striker William Ramallo scored a hat-trick; fellow striker Marco Etcheverry grabbed one; two goals fell to midfielder Erwin Sanchez, most outstanding graduate of the world-famous Bolivian kids' football academy, Tahuichi.

Next time out Bolivia beat Brazil 2-0 thanks to two goals in the last three minutes in La Paz and were on the roll which has taken them all the way to USA'94.

• *Three stars of Bolivia's World Cup run: Martinez (above), Melgar (left) and Ferrofino (below).*

THE MANAGER

XAVIER AZKARGORTA

Born September 29, 1953
Appointed March 1993

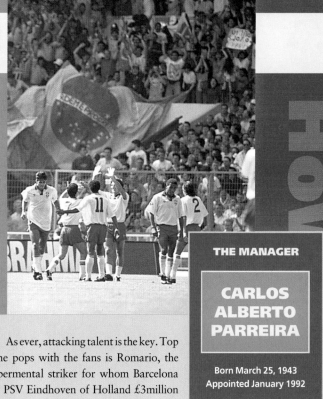

BRAZIL

Winners: 1958, 1962, 1970

Brazil are the greatest nation in World Cup history. Only Brazil have competed at every finals tournament.

Brazil were the first country to win the Cup three times. Brazil were the first nation – and remain the only one – to win the World Cup on the 'wrong' continent (in Sweden in 1958).

Brazil, above all, gave the World Cup Pele.

But that wondrous history has been sometimes more of a hindrance than a help to successive managerial predecessors of Carlos Alberto Parreira. The expectations of success among the torcida – the fans – back in Rio de Janeiro and Sao Paulo and the rest of a vast football-mad country are enormous. When Brazil were eliminated from the finals in 1982, 1986 and 1990, angry crowds thronged the main streets of the big cities burning effigies of the manager.

Carlos Alberto is determined that will not be his fate this time. Brazil did struggle in the qualifiers. It took a last-match victory over old enemies Uruguay to secure the necessary points. But no-one doubts that Brazil will be among the favourites to win a record fourth World Cup.

As ever, attacking talent is the key. Top of the pops with the fans is Romario, the tempermental striker for whom Barcelona paid PSV Eindhoven of Holland £3million last year. Injury spoiled Romario's ambitions in 1990, then he was overlooked for almost two years after a row with the manager. But Romario returned in glory with the two decisive goals which beat Uruguay.

Behind him and alongside are new heroes in Palhinha and the short-tempered Edmundo while the midfield is run by the tigerish Dunga, who plays in Germany with Stuttgart, and the sophisticated Rai, who plays in France with Paris Saint-Germain.

In 1992, Rai won the World Club Cup with Sao Paulo. Now he intends to be a World Cup-winner again ...

- *Top: Brazil celebrate a goal against England in 1992.*
- *Above left: Cafu (2), a brilliant full-back.*
- *Right: French-based midfielder Rai.*

THE MANAGER

CARLOS ALBERTO PARREIRA

Born March 25, 1943
Appointed January 1992

BRAZIL'S RESULTS
S. AMERICA GROUP B

0-0 v Ecuador
0-2 v Bolivia
5-1 v Venezuela
1-1 v Uruguay
2-0 v Ecuador
6-0 v Bolivia
4-0 v Venezuela
2-0 v Uruguay

S. AMERICA GROUP B FINAL TABLE

	P	W	D	L	F	A	Pts
Brazil	8	5	2	1	20	4	12
Bolivia	8	5	1	2	22	10	11
Uruguay	8	4	2	2	9	7	10
Ecuador	8	1	3	4	7	7	5
Venezuela	8	1	0	7	4	34	2

BULGARIA

Bulgaria left it to the very last seconds of the qualifying competition to claim their place at the World Cup finals

• *Bulgarian players celebrate beating France.*

EUROPEAN GROUP 6 FINAL TABLE

	P	W	D	L	F	A	Pts
Sweden	10	6	3	1	19	8	15
Bulgaria	10	6	2	2	19	10	14
France	10	6	1	3	17	10	13
Austria	10	3	2	5	15	16	8
Finland	10	2	1	7	9	18	5
Israel	10	1	3	6	10	27	5

in Spain with Valencia. Alongside Penev is another Spanish-based exile, Hristo Stoichkov. He was top scorer last year when Barcelona won their record third successive Spanish league title. Stoichkov is not only dangerous inside the penalty box, he rivals Barcelona team-mate Ronald Koeman of Holland when it comes to direct free kicks within range of goal.

This Bulgaria team can go forward confident about their security at the back where French-based Borislav Mikhailov, with more than 70 international appearances to his credit, will be one of the most experienced goalkeepers at USA'94. Helping out at the heart of defence is yet another of Bulgaria's foreign-based players, Trifon Ivanov, of Betis of Spain.

Manager Penev says: 'In the past we were afraid to play our football when we got to the finals. This time we intend to make everyone else afraid of us!'

A wonderful strike by centre-forward Emil Kostadinov brought a 2-1 victory in Paris over a shocked France who had thought they were home and dry.

Bulgaria first attended the finals in Chile in 1962. Over the years they have earned a reputation as a team of dour and relentless defence with few attackers of ability or class to lighten the gloom which surrounds their appearances in the international limelight.

But this Bulgarian team promise to be different under the managership of Dimiter Penev, a rock at the heart of Bulgaria's World Cup effort back in 1966, 1970 and 1974.

Penev's son, Lyubislav Penev, is one of Bulgaria and European football's outstanding footballers and knows all about big occasions from his three-year spell

BULGARIA'S RESULTS
EUROPEAN GROUP 6
3-0 v Finland
2-0 v France
0-2 v Sweden
2-0 v Israel
1-3 v Austria
2-0 v Finland
2-2 v Israel
1-1 v Sweden
4-1 v Austria
2-1 v France

• *More joy after the last-second victory in Paris.*

FIRST ROUND GROUP B FINAL TABLE	P	W	D	L	F	A	Pts
Cameroon	4	2	2	0	7	1	6
Swaziland	3	1	1	1	5	3	3
Zaire	3	0	1	2	1	3	1
Zaire v Swaziland	not played						

SECOND ROUND GROUP C FINAL TABLE	P	W	D	L	F	A	Pts
Cameroon	4	3	0	1	7	3	6
Zimbabwe	4	2	0	2	3	6	4
Guinea	4	1	0	3	4	5	2

CAMEROON

Back in the 1970s the veteran Brazilian commentator and coach, Joao Saldanha, made a daring prophesy.

THE MANAGER

HENRI MICHEL

Born October 28, 1947. Appointed January 1994

• *Cameroon's Denis Nde moves to tackle Zimbabwe's Sawli in the qualifying match which Zimbabwe won 1-0 in 1993.*

He predicted that a Black African nation would win the World Cup before the end of the century. Cameroon are the most likely team to bring Saldanha's vision to life.

No-one will forget the excitement and drama they brought to the 1990 finals in Italy. They defeated holders Argentina – Maradona and all – by 1-0 in the Opening Match, then went further than any other African nation by reaching the quarter-finals. They led England 2-1 before falling to two late penalties which cost them a semi-final place.

But even before 1990 Cameroon had been much more successful than many spectators realised. They have done well in African club competitions, where Canon and Tonnere of Yaounde have excelled, and in the African Championships they were runners-up to Egypt in 1986 and winners in 1988.

Their World Cup pedigree is good, too, for in their previous appearance in Spain, in 1982, they were unbeaten in their group matches, being eliminated only on the matter of goals scored by the eventual winners, Italy.

Among the outstanding players who have played for Cameroon are two former African Footballers of the Year, goalkeeper Thomas Nkono and Roger Milla, both stars of the 1990 World Cup challenge. Cameroon have rebuilt for the challenge of 1994.

Manager Leonard Nseke must look for many of his 'new' squad from among the players from the European leagues. François Omam Biyik, who began Cameroon's great run in the 1990 finals with that unforgettable winning goal in that Opening Match,will be brought from the French League where he has played for a number of clubs. Alongside him will be a new striker, Alphonse Tchami, who plays for Odense in Denmark. Goalkeeper Joseph-Antoine Bell is a veteran who was dropped for the 1990 campaign, went to France in 1985 and played for many other clubs before his current Saint-Etienne.

Cameroon will be strong and colourful again in 1994 and hoping to do at least as well as in 1982 and 1990.

CAMEROON'S RESULTS
SECOND ROUND GROUP C
3-1 v Guinea
0-1 v Zimbabwe
1-0 v Guinea
3-1 v Zimbabwe

CAMEROON'S RESULTS
FIRST ROUND GROUP B
5-0 v Swaziland
2-1 v Zaire
0-0 v Swaziland
0-0 v Zaire

THE MANAGER

FRANCISCO MATURANA

Born February 15, 1949
International player
for Colombia
Appointed January 1993
(for the second time)

COLOMBIA

Colombia were disappointed to have fallen at the second round to Cameroon in Italy four years ago.

• *The instantly recognisable Carlos Valderrama, Colombia's veteran midfield maestro.*

**COLOMBIA'S RESULTS
S. AMERICA
GROUP A**
0-0 v Paraguay
1-0 v Peru
2-1 v Argentina
1-1 v Paraguay
4-0 v Peru
5-0 v Argentina

This time, they believe, the support of thousands of their own fans in the United States will take them into the very closing stages.

Certainly they should prove one of the most attractive of competitors thanks to the explosive talents of forwards such as Faustino Asprilla and Adolfo Valencia, nicknamed The Train.

Colombia finished their qualifying campaign in glory in Buenos Aires. They went to Argentina needing a draw in their last game to secure their ticket to the United States. But Colombia did not go just to defend. They thrashed the hosts by an amazing 5-0 – one of the biggest defeats in Argentine history and a massive humiliation for the 1978 and 1986 World Cup holders.

Colombia's heroes in Buenos Aires were goalkeeper Oscar Cordoba, midfield general Carlos Valderrama and forwards Asprilla – who scored two of the five goals – Valencia and Fredy Rincon. In midfield Valderrama is familiar the world over, not only for his enormous ability but because of his mass of frizzy hair.

Asprilla, up front, is one of the new heroes of the international game. Few Colombians have moved abroad and to Europe, in particular, with success. But Asprilla made an instant impact when ambitious Italian club Parma signed him in the summer of 1992. Asprilla's goals inspired

Parma to reach the 1993 European Cup-winners' Cup Final, though he missed the Wembley victory over Belgium's Antwerp because of injury.

It was on the back of Asprilla's success that Parma will sign up national team partner Rincon after the World Cup finals. He will then be the third member of the Colombian attack in Europe: Adolfo Valencia was signed up by Bayern Munich after impressing the German club's spies at the 1993 South American championship (the Copa America).

• *Luis Carlos Perea with Germany's Augenthaler in the 1990 World Cup match, which was drawn 1-1.*

	P	W	D	L	F	A	Pts
S. AMERICA GROUP A FINAL TABLE							
Colombia	6	4	2	0	13	2	10
Argentina	6	3	1	2	7	9	7
Paraguay	6	1	4	1	6	7	6
Peru	6	0	1	5	4	12	1

• *Luis Herrera, a stalwart in Colombia's recent revival.*

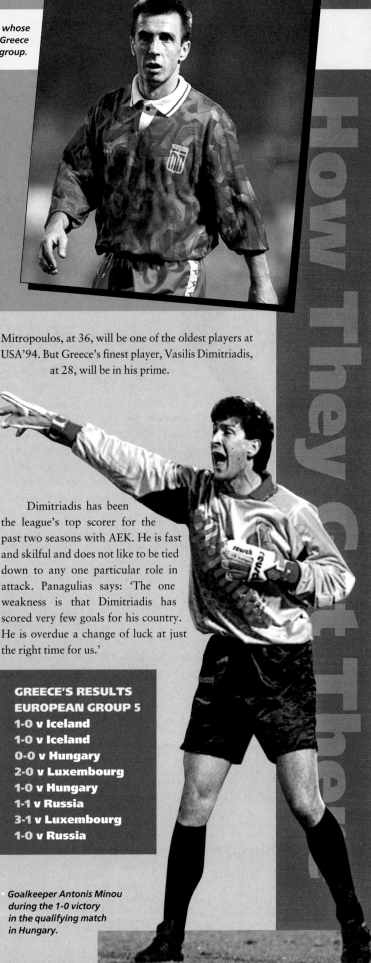

• Nicolaos Nioplias, whose performances helped Greece top their qualifying group.

GREECE

Greece are appearing at the peak of the world game for the first time in their history.

THE MANAGER

ALKETAS PANAGULIAS

Born May 30, 1934
30 international appearances
Appointed May 1992 (second time)

This is only the second occasion they have reached any major finals: the previous occasion was the finals of the European championship in Italy in 1980.

This time, fortune favoured the Greeks. They were drawn in the same qualifying group as Russia, Yugoslavia and Hungary plus minnows Iceland and Luxembourg. Between the draw, in New York in December 1991, and the start of matchplay, Yugoslavia had been suspended from all international football following the civil wars and Hungary had sunk into their worst post-war crisis.

By spring of 1993 Greece were left needing just one point from games against Russia (twice) and Luxembourg, to be sure of qualifying - which they accomplished with ease.

Manager Alketas Panagulias is the ideal man to lead Greece to the US since he has both studied and worked there. Now Panagulias says: 'The dark days have ended for Greek soccer. We have not conquered the world merely by qualifying for the finals and we need to work hard to justify our presence there but I can safely say we have opened the door for worldwide recognition.'

Veteran skills laid the foundations. Goalkeeper Antonis Minou, from champions AEK Athens, is 36, and defensive pillar Stelios Manolas, also from AEK, will be 34 during the finals. In midfield Tassos

Mitropoulos, at 36, will be one of the oldest players at USA'94. But Greece's finest player, Vasilis Dimitriadis, at 28, will be in his prime.

Dimitriadis has been the league's top scorer for the past two seasons with AEK. He is fast and skilful and does not like to be tied down to any one particular role in attack. Panagulias says: 'The one weakness is that Dimitriadis has scored very few goals for his country. He is overdue a change of luck at just the right time for us.'

GREECE'S RESULTS
EUROPEAN GROUP 5
1-0 v Iceland
1-0 v Iceland
0-0 v Hungary
2-0 v Luxembourg
1-0 v Hungary
1-1 v Russia
3-1 v Luxembourg
1-0 v Russia

• Goalkeeper Antonis Minou during the 1-0 victory in the qualifying match in Hungary.

EUROPEAN GROUP 5 FINAL TABLE

	P	W	D	L	F	A	Pts
Greece	8	6	2	0	10	2	14
Russia	8	5	2	1	15	5	12
Iceland	8	3	2	3	7	6	8
Hungary	8	2	1	5	6	10	5
Luxembourg	8	0	1	7	2	17	1

HOLLAND

Holland may be one of the smaller nations if you think strictly in terms of square kilometres.

• Ruud Gullit is hoping to return to the Dutch squad for the 1994 World Cup.

ow They ct Th e

EUROPEAN GROUP 2 FINAL TABLE

	P	W	D	L	F	A	Pts
Norway	10	7	2	1	25	5	16
Holland	10	6	3	1	29	9	15
England	10	5	3	2	26	9	13
Poland	10	3	2	5	10	15	8
Turkey	10	3	1	6	11	19	7
San Marino	10	0	1	9	2	46	1

But they are one of the giants of world football – an achievement which owes everything to the remarkable flowering of talent as bright and consistent as the tulips in the country's world famous bulb fields.

Qualification for USA'94 was not easily secured. As usual, the Dutch left the hard work for the last couple of matches. But the delight with which their qualifying success was greeted from Madrid to Moscow is proof that no-one has forgotten the great years of the early 1970s, when Johan Cruyff, Ajax and Holland thrilled the game at every level with the 'total football' which turned them into 1974 World Cup runners-up.

The Dutch federation hoped to persuade Cruyff to take over the team for the finals after Dick Advocaat had steered them through the qualifying round, but Advocaat remains in control. He hopes to take Holland one step further than their best efforts so far, when they were beaten Finalists in 1974 and 1978. He has the talent available to do it.

Ronald Koeman is not only a solid centre-back, he is one of the most powerful free-kick experts in the world – as England know only too well from Rotterdam. Frank Rijkaard in midfield refined his match-reading abilities with Milan in Italy where his partnership with Ruud Gullit and Marco Van Basten was feared throughout Europe.

Gullit's presence at USA '94 depends on his making his peace with Advocaat after falling out with him last year, but Van Basten is unlikely to be there because of long-standing ankle trouble. But it says everything about the wonder of Dutch football that a new super-star has blossomed in Dennis Bergkamp, once of Ajax and now in Italy with Internazionale. The service provided by wingers Marc Overmars and Brian Roy might even turn Bergkamp into . . . the new Cruyff!

THE MANAGER

DICK ADVOCAAT

Born Sept 27, 1947
Appointed September 1992

HOLLAND'S RESULTS EUROPEAN GROUP 2

1-2 v Norway	2-2 v England
2-2 v Poland	0-0 v Norway
3-1 v Turkey	7-0 v San Marino
3-1 v Turkey	2-0 v England
6-0 v San Marino	3-1 v Poland

• Peter Van Vossen scores from a penalty to earn Holland a 2-2 draw in their qualifying match in England.

ITALY

Winners: 1934, 1938, 1982

For many prominent figures , and ordinary fans alike, Italy is the centre of world football.

THE MANAGER

ARRIGO SACCHI

Born April 1, 1946
Appointed October 1991

• *Paolo Maldini, Italy's brilliant full-back, tackles Scotland's Derek Whyte in 1992.*

With Milan, Sacchi had revealed himself as a quiet revolutionary. He had scrapped the old man-to-man marking and dominated Italian, European and world club football by using a zone defence and 'pressing' tactics. Milan's support work for the man on the ball was exemplary and, of course, the big-money purchases of Ruud Gullit and Marco Van Basten provided an attacking edge to their game no-one else could match.

Now Sacchi takes Italy to the United States confident in his methods and in his men: that is not surprising, given that the backbone of his Italy were his pupils at Milan.

Sweeper Franco Baresi has, for several years, been acknowledged the best in the world; left-back Paolo Maldini possesses all the talent handed down from his father, Cesare, who captained Milan to European Cup success in the 1960s; in midfield the likes of Stefano Eranio and Demetrio Albertini provide ideal support for the attacking talents of Juventus' Roberto Baggio.

Recently voted European Footballer of the Year, Baggio is the outstanding individual talent of the day. Juventus paid a then world record £8million for him three years ago. Now all that potential may be fulfilled with Italy's record fourth World Cup.

While officials elsewhere in Europe have been worrying about mounting debts and falling attendances and television competition, Italian football has established itself ever more securely as the centre of the world game. Italy's three World Cup victories – in 1934, 1938 and 1982 say everything about the strength of Calcio.

Not that the fans saw things that way when Italy lost on penalties to Argentina in Naples in the semi-finals of 'their own' World Cup finals four years ago. The hangover continued through the qualifying rounds of the 1992 European championship. Even before the preliminary matches had been completed, failed manager Azeglio Vicini handed over control to Arrigo Sacchi.

EUROPEAN GROUP 1 FINAL TABLE

	P	W	D	L	F	A	Pts
Italy	10	7	2	1	22	7	16
Switzerland	10	6	3	1	23	6	15
Portugal	10	6	2	2	18	5	14
Scotland	10	4	3	3	14	13	11
Malta	10	1	1	8	3	23	3
Estonia	10	0	1	9	1	27	1

ITALY'S RESULTS EUROPEAN GROUP 1

2-2 v Switzerland
0-0 v Scotland
2-1 v Malta
3-1 v Portugal
6-1 v Malta
2-0 v Estonia
0-1 v Switzerland
3-0 v Estonia
3-1 v Scotland
1-0 v Portugal

THE MANAGER

MIGUEL MEJIA BARON

Born September 6, 1944
Appointed December 1992

MEXICO

MEXICO became the first nation to qualify for the finals when they won 2-1 in Canada in May last year.

MEXICO'S RESULTS N.& CENT. AMERICA 2ND ROUND, GP A

4-0 v St Vincent
2-0 v Honduras
4-0 v Costa Rica
0-2 v Costa Rica
11-0 v St Vincent
1-1 v Honduras

MEXICO'S RESULTS FINAL ROUND

1-2 v El Salvador
3-0 v Honduras
3-1 v El Salvador
4-0 v Canada
4-1 v Honduras
2-1 v Canada

Nothing less than instant qualification was their goal after the disappointment of the 1990 World Cup from which Mexico were barred by FIFA as punishment for fielding over-age players in a World Youth Cup qualifying event.

Mexico's greatest memories concern the fact that they were the first nation to stage the World Cup finals twice. The first hosting was the wonderful event of 1970, the second the memorable tournament of 1986. Apart from these obvious occasions, Mexico have become almost permanent visitors to the finals. The reason lies in the weak opposition surrounding them in central and North America. Qualification has always been comparatively easy.

This time the federation took no chances and signed up Cesar Luis Menotti, manager of Argentina's 1978 World Cup-winners, to run their qualifying campaign. But Menotti was a casualty of political in-fighting within the Mexican federation so the challenge fell to his erstwhile No 2, Miguel Mejia Baron.

Like veteran striker Hugo Sanchez, Mejia Baron originally qualified outside football as a dentist and intended going into practice when his playing career with top club America had finished. Instead he was persuaded to try his hand at management.

Mejia Baron has welded together a team of characters. They start with goalkeeper Jorge Campos, famous for his multi-coloured kit and for the fact that he is also more than useful as a striker. Miguel Espana, a 1986 veteran, is still around to bring the weight of experience to midfield while Hugo Sanchez and Zague promise goals a-plenty up front.

Zague, son of a Brazilian star of the same name, set a modern-day international record when he scored seven goals in a Central and North American qualifying tie last year.

Left: Mexican midfielder Ignacio Ambriz demonstrates a sound first touch during a recent Copa America game.

N. & CENT. AMERICA 2ND ROUND GP A FINAL TABLE

	P	W	D	L	F	A	Pts
Mexico	6	4	1	1	22	3	9
Honduras	6	4	1	1	14	6	9
Costa Rica	6	3	0	3	11	9	6
St Vincent	6	0	0	6	0	29	0

N. & CENT. AMERICA GP A FINAL ROUND TABLE

	P	W	D	L	F	A	Pts
Mexico	6	5	0	1	17	5	10
Canada	6	3	1	2	10	10	7
El Salvador	6	2	0	4	6	11	4
Honduras	6	1	1	4	7	14	3

MOROCCO

Morocco's World Cup ambitions include becoming the first African nation to host the World Cup finals.

MOROCCO'S
RESULTS
AFRICA FIRST
ROUND GP F
5-0 v Ethiopia
1-0 v Benin
1-1 v Tunisia
1-0 v Ethiopia
5-0 v Benin
0-0 v Tunisia

Morocco will be appearing in their third World Cup finals in 1994, having established a reputation in 1970 and 1986 of being determined opponents who are difficult to beat. In 1970, Morocco were the first African nation to appear in the World Cup finals since the war (Egypt played a single match in 1934). They took the challenge seriously, training in the Atlas mountains to prepare themselves for the altitude of Mexico. It looked as if they might bring off one of the biggest shocks of all time when in their first match they led West Germany 1-0 at half-time. It was no disgrace when they lost 2-1. A draw with Bulgaria sent them home happy.

The Moroccan Championship dates back to 1916, but the game developed apace after independence in 1956, with encouragement from King Hassan, who backed the Forces Armees Royales team of Rabat. FAR eventually won the African Nations Cup in the 1980s in time for their Brazilian coach, Jose Faria, to take over the coaching of the national team and take them to the finals of the World Cup in 1986. In the meantime, Morocco reached the quarter-finals of the Olympic tournament in 1972 and won the African Nations Cup in 1976 with a 5-4 defeat of Guinea. Their best player, Ahmed Faras, was African Footballer of the Year.

Morocco did very well in the 1986 World Cup. Draws with Poland and England and a 3-1 defeat of Portugal took them to the second round, where again West Germany were their nemesis – but the Europeans, who were to reach the Final, won only with a last-minute free-kick which just crept in.

• An airborne Lahcen Abrami of Morocco clears under pressure from a Zambian forward during Morocco's 1-0 victory in the African second round qualifiers.

Under their new manager, Abdellah Blinda, Morocco won their first qualifying group for 1994 after a struggle with Tunisia, with whom they drew twice. Neither side lost a match, but Tunisia's draw with Ethiopia deprived them of the place in the final qualifying group.

Here Morocco's rivals were Zambia, the tragic side of USA'94. Practically the entire Zambia squad were wiped out in an air-crash in 1993. But, in sorrow and pride, Zambia rebuilt their side and inflicted on Morocco their first defeat of the campaign. Morocco played Zambia in the return needing to win to go to the USA, and a late goal gave them a place by 1-0.

Morocco will be looking to improve their already respectable record in the finals. They will rely on their French connection to form the bedrock of the side: midfielders Mohamed Chaouch of Nice and Mustafa El-Haddaoui of Angers. Nancy's Mustapha Hadji, picked for the French Under-21 team, elected instead to play for Morocco, hoping for a World Cup place.

Optimism is the key-word for Morocco. They were the first African nation to apply to host the World Cup, trying for the 1994 and 1998 tournaments. They hope to be pioneers.

MOROCCO'S RESULTS SECOND ROUND GP B

1-0 v Senegal
1-2 v Zambia
3-1 v Senegal
1-0 v Zambia

AFRICA FIRST ROUND GP F FINAL TABLE

	P	W	D	L	F	A	Pts
Morocco	6	4	2	0	13	1	10
Tunisia	6	3	3	0	14	2	9
Ethiopia	6	1	1	4	3	11	3
Benin	6	1	0	5	3	19	2

AFRICA SECOND ROUND GP B FINAL TABLE

	P	W	D	L	F	A	Pts
Morocco	4	3	0	1	6	3	6
Zambia	4	2	1	1	6	2	5
Senegal	4	0	1	3	1	8	1

NIGERIA

World Cup qualification was the second triumph in a matter of weeks last year for Nigeria.

THE MANAGER

CLEMENTS WESTERHOF

Born March 3, 1940, in Holland
Appointed February 1991
(for the second time)

Their juniors won the World Under-17 Cup last August when they defeated fellow Africans and defending title-holders Ghana in the Final. That success was a good omen for the real thing, according to youth coach Fanny Ikhayere Amun.

He said: 'I am convinced that African countries could win the senior World Cup by 2002. The ability is here. The ambition is here. It is merely a matter of time.'

One key factor in the qualifying campaign was the ambition of key players such as captain Stephen Keshi, fellow defender Augustine Eguavon and forwards Rashidi Yekini – five-goal overall top scorer in the African qualifying section – and Samson Siasia. This was their last chance of appearing in the finals and they were determined not to miss it.

Nigeria have traditionally benefited from an abundance of talented young players. The contributions of new stars such as Jay-Jay Okocha (the Eintracht Frankfurt midfielder), fullback Nduka Ugbade and forwards Emmanuel Amunike,

• *Above: Nigeria's chunky Nduka 'Duke' Ubade and (below) Alloy Agu, the last line in a defence that did not concede a goal during the first round qualifying games.*

Monaco's Victor Ikpeba and Brugge's Daniel Amokachi have been immense.

The fixture schedule worked to their advantage with a last qualifying tie against an Algerian side who were already out of the race and low on morale. Thus Nigeria had few problems and secured the necessary point from a 1-1 draw. Finidi George, who plays his club football for top European club Ajax Amsterdam, scored the all-important goal.

Nigeria was introduced to football by the British, the Football Association was set up in 1945 but, as yet, Nigeria have never won the African Nations Cup nor have any of their players ever been celebrated as African Footballer of the Year. Failings at senior level, however, have been widely compensated by Nigeria's success in twice winning the World Under-17 Cup.

NIGERIA'S RESULTS AFRICA FIRST ROUND GP D

4-0 v South Africa
1-0 v Congo
0-0 v South Africa
2-0 v Congo

NIGERIA'S RESULTS SECOND ROUND GP A

1-2 v Ivory Coast
4-1 v Algeria
4-1 v Ivory Coast
1-1 v Algeria

AFRICA FIRST ROUND GP D FINAL TABLE

	P	W	D	L	F	A	Pts
Nigeria	4	3	1	0	7	0	7
South Africa	4	2	1	1	2	4	5
Congo	4	0	0	4	0	5	0

SECOND ROUND GP A FINAL TABLE

	P	W	D	L	F	A	Pts
Nigeria	4	2	1	1	10	5	5
Ivory Coast	4	2	1	1	5	6	5
Algeria	4	0	2	2	3	7	2

How They Go

NORWAY

A brilliant late equaliser earned Norway a vital point in their match with England at Wembley.

However, for the English, the great upset about Norway's World Cup presence is that most of their key men play league football in England and that manager Egil Olsen claims it was using 'the traditional direct English game' which enabled them to beat both Holland and England.

Until the recent qualifying dramatics, Norway's greatest achievement had been in collecting the bronze medal at the 1936 Berlin Olympics. Now Olsen has set about putting Norway back on the world football map – together, of course, with support from Spurs' Erik Thorstvedt, Liverpool defender Stig Inge Bjornbye, Oldham midfielder Gunnar Halle and strikers Jostein Flo (Sheffield United) and Jan Age Fjortoft (Swindon).

Goalkeeper Thorstvedt is one of the most experienced internationals in Norway's history with more than 80 international appearances. In front is sweeper Rune Bratseth of German club Werder Bremen, Norway's most complete footballer of all time. He is the defensive "commander" of both club and country and helped Bremen beat Monaco in the 1992 European Cup-winners' Cup Final. Thus he knows all about the big occasion.

Midfielder Halle is another member of the English connection who has regained his form and fitness after injury and was followed across the North Sea by Kare Ingebrigtsen and Lars Bohinen.

Up front, Fjortoft was a fixture in the national team long before the recent glory years and his 14 goals in 30-plus internationals earned a transfer to Austria with Rapid Vienna. Inconsistency later let him down but Fjortoft remains assured of a place in Norwegian football history for the goal which earned a 1-1 draw against Brazil in July 1988.

That result was hailed as a triumph in its own right – but one which pales into comparative insignificance compared with what these Norwegians have now achieved in qualifying for USA'94.

- *Above left: Goran Sorloth celebrating the home win over England and (left) tussling for possession with Gary Pallister.*
- *Above: Bohinen takes on David Platt.*

THE MANAGER

EGIL OLSEN

Born April 22, 1942
16 international appearances
Appointed 1990

NORWAY'S RESULTS
EUROPEAN GROUP 2

10-0 v San Marino
2-1 v Holland
2-0 v San Marino
1-1 v England
3-1 v Turkey
2-0 v England
0-0 v Holland
1-0 v Poland
3-0 v Poland
1-2 v Turkey

EUROPEAN GROUP 2 FINAL TABLE							
	P	W	D	L	F	A	PTS
Norway	10	7	2	1	25	5	16
Holland	10	6	3	1	29	9	15
England	10	5	3	2	26	9	13
Poland	10	3	2	5	10	15	8
Turkey	10	3	1	6	11	19	7
San Marino	10	0	1	9	2	46	1

REPUBLIC OF

Little more than six years ago the Republic of Ireland had never appeared on centre stage at major international level.

• Left: Andy Townsend directing events in midfied.

Now they're old stagers, finalists at the 1988 European championships in Germany, at the World Cup in Italy in 1990 and now, again, at the 1994 jamboree.

For years the Republic's national team had been one of Europe's minnows. They stood little higher than Finland in the international rankings. Talented players, such as Johnny Giles and then Liam Brady, earned critical acclaim in European club competition. But at national team level . . . nothing.

Then the Football Association of Ireland had the bright idea of appointing Jack Charlton as manager. He had been overlooked in the past for the England job and had proved an effective and successful club manager with Middlesbrough and Sheffield Wednesday. England's loss proved to be Ireland's gain.

Charlton insisted he did not want to be a full-time manager. He wanted time in the week to pursue his other sporting interests. The time he spent huntin', shootin' and fishin' only served, however, to sharpen his pursuit of a different sort of game – football.

Charlton's arrival at the helm saw the activation of two distinct policies. One was to hunt down all the best players who had missed international selection for England or Scotland but who still qualified for the Irish Republic through the birth qualification of parents or grandparents. Secondly, Charlton formulated a simple and effective style based on solid defence, and a midfield who stifled the life out of opponents before seeking the most direct of attacking options.

New players found it comparatively easy to fit into the game plan while the team spirit engendered by

IRELAND

THE MANAGER

JACK CHARLTON

Born May 8, 1936
35 international appearances for England –
including the 1966 World Cup victory
Appointed, 1986

this great Irish adventure proved additionally infectious. Pat Bonner in goal, Paul McGrath in defence then Ronnie Whelan, Andy Townsend and Ray Houghton in midfield all earned rave reviews for their individual exploits.

At the 1988 European championship finals the Irish beat England 1-0 in the first game and came within a few minutes of a place in the semi-finals. A late goal by Holland's Wim Kieft in Gelsenkirchen ended Irish dreams in the first round. But the green-garbed fans went home in high spirits.

So they did again two years later when the Irish Republic emerged from a first-round group matching them with both England and Holland again, defeated Romania on penalties in the second round – Bonner was the hero of the day – then lost only 1-0 to Italy in the quarter-finals.

Narrow failure in the qualifiers for the next European championship followed. But suggestions that the green bubble had burst were quickly dispelled in the qualifying rounds for a place at USA'94. Denmark, Spain and Northern Ireland presented testing opposition. Indeed, after a 3-1 home defeat by Spain last October, it appeared the Irish might not make it.

But their luck held. On the last, dramatic, match-day, the Republic drew 1-1 away to Northern Ireland in Belfast yet owed their place in the vital top two places thanks to Denmark's 1-0 defeat in Spain. Thus

the toast, in Dublin's bars on the night of Wednesday November 17, was to an American World Cup, to Jack Charlton but, above all, to the most unlikely Irish hero of all . . . Spain's Fernando Hierro.

• *Far left: John Sheridan takes on the Spanish defence. Below: Ray Houghton snatches a quick breather.*

REPUBLIC OF

HOW TH...

Roy Keane moves into top gear against Northern Ireland.

Right: Niall Quinn celebrates his goal against Denmark.

EUROPEAN GROUP 3 FINAL TABLE

	P	W	D	L	F	A	Pts
Spain	12	8	3	1	27	4	19
Rep Ireland	12	7	4	1	19	6	18
Denmark	12	7	4	1	15	2	18
N Ireland	12	5	3	4	14	13	13
Lithuania	12	2	3	7	8	21	7
Latvia	12	0	5	7	4	21	5
Albania	12	1	2	9	6	26	4

IRELAND

THE IRISH WAY

Dublin's College Park was the venue for the first recorded match in southern Ireland. That was on November 7, 1883, when Dublin University played Dublin Association.

The Football Association of Ireland was founded on June 1, 1921, after the partition of Ireland. Northern Ireland maintained the Irish Football Association designation.

The Irish Free State, as they were then termed, lost 3-0 to Italy in Turin in their first-ever international match on March 21, 1926.

Liam Brady, with 72 caps, is Ireland's record international after a national team career lasting 15 years from 1975 to 1990.

Ireland's record international marksman is Frank Stapleton, with 20 goals scored in 70 matches between 1977 and 1990. Stapleton won selection while playing for 6 different clubs – Arsenal, Manchester United, Ajax Amsterdam, Derby County, Le Havre and Blackburn Rovers.

• Left: All dressed up but not much to cel-ebrate against Spain in 1993.

How They Got T

ROMANIA

Romania made a winning start to their campaign when they beat the Faroe Islands 7-0 in Bucharest in May 1992.

THE MANAGER

ANGHEL IORDANESCU

Born May 4, 1950
26 international appearances. Appointed June 1993

They finally rounded off a successful campaign by winning 2-1 away to Wales in Cardiff.

In between their form occasionally faltered. But few observers doubt they possess the quality to go beyond the second round which proved their stopping point in Italy four years ago. For one thing, many of Romania's players have taken advantage of the opening up of the Iron Curtain to seek fame, fortune – and vital big-occasion experience – abroad.

Chief among these are the three men central to Romania's World Cup bid: Gica Popescu, Gheorghe Hagi in midfield and Florin Raducioiu up front. All were on board at Italia'90. Popescu, from PSV Eindhoven, is one of the best sweepers in Europe; Hagi, with Italian club Brescia, is one of the most exciting and inventive of attacking midfielders; and Raducioiu's marksman talents have been honed this past season with Italian champions Milan.

Organising and controlling them is manager Anghel Iordanescu, appointed last summer to replace ex-World Cup stopper Cornel Dinu after a 5-2 defeat by Czechoslovakia.

Iordanescu leans heavily on Romania's foreign legion in his squad selection. At least half of his regular squad of 22 men are with foreign clubs in Italy, Spain, Belgium and Holland. The remaining 11 players are drawn from a domestic nucleus of Steaua, Dinamo Bucharest and Universitatea Craiova. One of the Steaua players, veteran striker Marius Lacatus, has only just returned home after a spell in Spain.

Lacatus says: 'In Italy we were overwhelmed by the atmosphere and the pressure. Now we know what the World Cup is all about and we are ready for it!'

Above: Albert (Belgium) and Dumitrescu (Romania) both look determined to claim the ball.

Left: Florin Raducioiu and Rudi Smits of Belgium battle for the ball during Romania's hard fought 2-1 victory in the October 1993 qualifier.

ROMANIA'S RESULTS EUROPEAN GROUP 4

7-0 v Faroe Islands
5-1 v Wales
0-1 v Belgium
1-1 v Czechoslovakia
4-1 v Cyprus
2-1 v Cyprus
2-5 v Czechoslovakia
4-0 v Faroe Islands
2-1 v Belgium
2-1 v Wales

EUROPEAN GROUP 4 FINAL TABLE

	P	W	D	L	F	A	Pts
Romania	10	7	1	2	29	12	15
Belgium	10	7	1	2	16	5	15
Czechoslovakia	10	4	5	1	21	9	13
Wales	10	5	2	3	19	12	12
Cyprus	10	2	1	7	8	18	5
Faroe Islands	10	0	0	10	1	38	0

RUSSIA

Russia compete in the World Cup finals for the first time – the old USSR having collapsed in 1991.

• Right: Russian 'keeper Kharin directs his defence from the goalmouth.

THE MANAGER

PAVEL SADYRIN

Born September 18, 1942. Appointed July, 1992

EUROPEAN GROUP 5 FINAL TABLE	P	W	D	L	F	A	Pts
Greece	8	6	2	0	10	2	14
Russia	8	5	2	1	15	4	12
Iceland	8	3	2	3	7	6	8
Hungary	8	2	1	5	6	11	5
Luxembourg	8	0	1	7	2	17	1
Yugoslavia suspended from participation							

Its sporting remnants, the CIS – or, Commonwealth of Independent States – wound up the Soviet sporting era at the 1992 European championship finals.

After that, the various republics of the old USSR went their separate ways. But one, Russia, had an inbuilt advantage. Its central role at the heart of the Soviet Union meant it had been granted the right to take over the Soviets' place in the draw for the 1994 World Cup qualifiers.

Ukraine, Belorussia and Georgia all had to wait until next time. But Russia went straight into a preliminary group already weakened by the suspension of Yugoslavia and, by June of last year, had secured their place in the finals.

Traditionally, the Soviets began every finals tournament at high speed but failed to last the pace – even in 1966, when they achieved their best-ever fourth position. The last time the World Cup finals were held in the Americas, in Mexico, the Soviets started with a whirlwind six-goal demolition of Hungary ... then ran out of steam against Belgium in the second round.

Manager Pavel Sadyrin is determined to learn from these mistakes, saying: 'What happened before was down to insufficient experience among our coaches. This time, we will be much better prepared not only physically but mentally as well.'

Previously, Sadyrin coached CSKA Moscow and his goalkeeper with the Red Army team, Dimitri Kharin (now Chelsea), will be an automatic choice for the World Cup squad. So will the 1992 Footballer of the Year Viktor Onopko, a left-side midfield player who captained Moscow Spartak to two successive championships.

In attack Sergei Yuran and Andrei Kanchelskis abandoned their Ukraine origins to opt to continue their international careers with Russia while Spartak's Vladimir Beschastnikh is Russia's new 'wonderboy'.

• Right: Russian attacker Kolyvanov looks comfortable on the ball as he moves forward in attack during the 1-0 defeat of Iceland in the European Group 3 qualifiers.

RUSSIA'S RESULTS EUROPEAN GROUP 5

1-0 v Iceland
2-0 v Luxembourg
4-0 v Luxembourg
3-0 v Hungary
1-1 v Greece
1-1 v Iceland
3-1 v Hungary
0-1 v Greece

SAUDI ARABIA

Saudi Arabia will be welcome newcomers at the World Cup finals – their presence a long overdue return on investment.

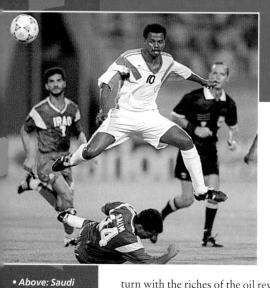

**SAUDI ARABIA'S RESULTS
ASIA FIRST ROUND GP E**
6-0 v Macao
1-1 v Malaysia
0-0 v Kuwait
8-0 v Macao
3-0 v Malaysia
2-0 v Kuwait

**SAUDI ARABIA'S
RESULTS
SECOND ROUND**
0-0 v Japan
2-1 v N Korea
1-1 v S Korea
1-1 v Iraq
4-2 v Iran

• *Above: Saudi Arabia's Saeed Owairin hurdles an Iraqi defender during the second round qualifying tournament in Qatar.*

The long history of sporting enthusiasms in the Gulf States – falconry, camel racing – took a western turn with the riches of the oil revolution.

When the Saudi government announced a youth welfare programme in 1976, football became a new passion. Millions of pounds were poured into sports centres and indoor stadiums. The football federation was allowed to bring in foreign managers and coaches, and could afford the best. A succession of British, German and Brazilian coaches went to Saudi Arabia.

Although Saudi clubs did well in Asian competition it was not until 1989 that success arrived at the national level with the World Junior (under-17) Championship, won in Scotland.

Brazilian coach Carlos Alberto Parreira failed to get Saudi Arabia to the World Cup finals of 1990, however, and left to manage the United Arab Emirates in 1990 on his way to managing Brazil in 1994.

The new manager, Jose Candido, took Saudi Arabia to the final Asian qualifying tournament in Qatar, but after an argument with the federation paymasters he was dismissed midway through. The new coach, who will take Saudi Arabia to the USA, is Leo Beenhakker, from Rotterdam, who managed the Dutch national team in the 1990 finals and has coached such club giants as Ajax Amsterdam and Real Madrid.

Saudi Arabia won through to Qatar with an impressive performance in their first group, where they were unbeaten and squeezed through at the expense of Kuwait. The Qatar tournament, played over two weeks in Doha, pitted them against Iraq, Iran, North and South Korea and Japan in a shoot-out for two places.

Saudi were without their veteran star Majid Mohammed, who was badly injured early on, but at least had the support of hundreds of fans who made the trip over the border to cheer the side on.

It was a very close and exciting tournament. The Saudis began with a 0-0 draw with Japan, then beat North Korea 2-1. Two more draws, 1-1, meant that they played their last match against Iran knowing that a win would give them one of the places in the USA.

The fans went wild as the Saudis won 4-2. The goalscorers, Sami Al Jaber, Fahad Mehalel, Mansour Al Mosa and Hamzah Falatah, were heroes and will be expected to score more goals in the USA. But the star was goalkeeper Mohammed Al-Deayea, with outstanding performances throughout the tournament. He will be one of a number of veteran 'keepers doing their stuff in the USA. All Saudi Arabia will look to him and Beenhakker for a good run in the finals.

ASIA 1ST ROUND GP E FINAL TABLE

	P	W	D	L	F	A	Pts
Saudi Arabia	6	4	2	0	20	1	10
Kuwait	6	3	2	1	21	4	8
Malaysia	6	2	2	2	16	7	6
Macao	6	0	0	6	1	46	0

ASIA SECOND ROUND FINAL TABLE

	P	W	D	L	F	A	Pts
Saudi Arabia	5	2	3	0	8	5	7
South Korea	5	2	2	1	9	4	6
Japan	5	2	2	1	7	4	6
Iraq	5	1	3	1	9	9	5
Iran	5	2	0	3	7	11	4
North Korea	5	1	0	4	5	12	2

SOUTH KOREA

South Korea have reached the World Cup finals three times in a row and four times in all.

ASIA 1ST ROUND GP D FINAL TABLE							
	P	W	D	L	F	A	Pts
South Korea	8	7	1	0	22	0	15
Bahrain	8	3	3	2	9	6	9
Lebanon	8	2	4	2	8	9	8
Hong Kong	8	2	1	5	8	18	5
India	8	1	1	6	8	22	3

ASIA SECOND ROUND FINAL TABLE							
	P	W	D	L	F	A	Pts
Saudi Arabia	5	2	3	0	8	5	7
South Korea	5	2	2	1	9	4	6
Japan	5	2	2	1	7	4	6
Iraq	5	1	3	1	9	9	5
Iran	5	2	0	3	7	11	4
North Korea	5	1	0	4	5	12	2

South Korea squeezed into the finals of the 1994 World Cup, getting there by a last-second effort by a player at another venue.

This was at the desert shoot-out of the Asian nations in Qatar, where South Korea's narrow squeak contrasted greatly with their regal progress through their first group. With Bahrain, Lebanon, Hong Kong and India as their rivals, South Korea dropped a point in a 0-0 draw in their first match but won all the rest, scoring 22 goals without conceding one.

South Korea went to Qatar with high hopes, but a 1-0 defeat by Japan seemed to have dashed them. On the last day Japan and Saudi Arabia needed only to win their matches to win places in the USA. South Korea gave themselves every chance by beating North Korea 3-0, but with both Saudi Arabia and Japan winning it seemed too late. South Korea had already finished their match and were in subdued mood until news arrived that with seconds left Iraq had scored an equalizer against Japan. Unbelievably, they were through.

This improved South Korea's World Cup record to the best of those of the emergent soccer nations – it is the third consecutive time and fourth in all that they have reached the finals. As long ago as 1954 they played in Switzerland, but were beaten 9-0 and 7-0 by Hungary and Turkey respectively. In 1986 and 1990 they achieved no more than a draw with Bulgaria, but none of their defeats was by more than two goals and

they played such giants as Argentina (3-1), Italy (3-2) and Spain (3-1).

Ho Kim, who took over as manager after the 1990 finals, promised that South Korea would be in the USA in 1994 but could hardly have expected them to leave it to the last ten seconds. The goalscorers in the vital match, Hwang Sun-hong, Ko Jeung-woon and Ha Seok-ju, will be vital players in 1994. Hwang Sun-hong is a striker who played in the 1990 finals when the failure of both Asian nations to get past the first round spoiled the chances of a place for a third Asian representative in the 1994 finals.

However, such is the upbeat feeling in South Korean football at their progress that they believe they might have an automatic place in the 2002 finals – as hosts.

THE MANAGER

HO KIM

Born March 17, 1944
50 international appearances
Appointed September 1990

S. KOREA'S RESULTS
ASIA FIRST ROUND GP D
0-0 v Bahrain
1-0 v Lebanon
3-0 v India
3-0 v Hong Kong
3-0 v Hong Kong
2-0 v Lebanon
7-0 v India
3-0 v Bahrain

S. KOREA'S RESULTS
SECOND ROUND
3-0 v Iran
2-2 v Iraq
1-1 v Saudi Arabia
0-1 v Japan
3-0 v North Korea

Above: Jang Yoon Nol fills a South Korean sandwich as two Japanese defenders converge.

SPAIN

Spain mean business this time. Previously, all their honours – bar one – have been seized by their great clubs like Real Madrid and Barcelona.

EUROPEAN GROUP 3 FINAL TABLE							
	P	W	D	L	F	A	Pts
Spain	12	8	3	1	27	4	19
Rep Ireland	12	7	4	1	19	6	18
Denmark	12	7	4	1	15	2	18
N Ireland	12	5	3	4	14	13	13
Lithuania	12	2	3	7	8	21	7
Latvia	12	0	5	7	4	21	5
Albania	12	1	2	9	6	26	4

SPAIN'S RESULTS
EUROPEAN GROUP 3

3-0 v Albania	0-1 v Denmark
0-0 v Latvia	3-1 v N Ireland
0-0 v N Ireland	2-0 v Lithuania
0-0 v Rep Ireland	5-1 v Albania
5-0 v Latvia	3-1 v Rep Ireland
5-0 v Lithuania	1-0 v Denmark

Now, finally, the national team have come out of the shadows and plan to go one better than in 1964, when they won the European Championship.

The man who has given Spain new confidence, belief and drawn new interest and enthusiasm among the fans is Javier Clemente. The former Bilbao midfielder had, for years, been the obvious candidate. But the complex politics of Spanish football had meant his appointment had needed to wait for the accession of a fellow Basque, Angel Villar, to the presidency of the FEF.

Clemente immediately set about rebuilding Spain in the image of Barcelona. To the irritation of Barcelona coach Johan Cruyff, Clemente selected six, seven and eight Barsa players in his squads while virtually ignoring the players of Real Madrid.

Andoni Zubizarreta has proved immovable in goal – until, that is, he was sent off in the dramatic, climactic 1-0 defeat of Denmark in the qualifying competition. Earlier, in the 3-1 victory over the Irish Republic in Dublin, 'Zubi' equalled Jose Camacho's record of 81 international appearances for Spain.

In front of Zubizarreta are plenty of friendly Barcelona faces such as the aggressive fullback Jose Ferrer, highly-rated midfielder Josep Guardiola, creative dynamo Jose Maria Bakero and lanky striker Julio Salinas. Remarkably, Salinas rattled home a succession of vital goals – three away to Albania, two in Ireland – while simultaneously failing to find a spot anywhere but on the substitutes' bench at Barcelona.

Spain's record of World Cup disappointments means they will go to USA'94 without suffering from excessive complacency and without the burdens of enormous expectation among their fans. They could thus be at their most dangerous.

• *Top: Spanish players mob Julio Salinas after the Barcelona player had scored the second against Ireland.*
• *Below: Fernando Hierro rises above it all in Dublin.*

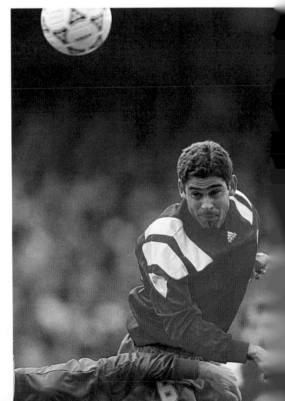

THE MANAGER

JAVIER CLEMENTE

Born March 12, 1950
Appointed July, 1992

SWEDEN

Sweden manager Tommy Svensson believes Santa Claus is bringing Sweden to the World Cup finals.

THE MANAGER

TOMMY SVENSSON

Born March 4, 1945. 40 international appearances
Appointed 1990

Sweden headed their group but could hardly believe their luck at the fall of France.

A 3-2 victory over the comparatively weak Finland in October was an unimpressive effort, but France's home collapse to two late goals by Israel meant Sweden's place in the finals was secure.

But manager Tommy Svensson knows that if Sweden are not to have as disappointing a time as in 1990, when they were fancied outsiders but lost all their three games 2-1, he has many problems to sort out. Two of his leading players, midfielder Jonas Thern and striker Tomas Brolin, have been injured or out of form or both.

Sweden's glory days in the World Cup began in 1950. Having finished third to Uruguay and Brazil in the finals, Sweden hosted the tournament in 1958 and reached the Final, where they lost 5-2 to Brazil and the 17-year-old genius of Pele.

Most of Sweden's top players have always had to seek their fortunes abroad, as the amateur ethic was deeply entrenched at that time. Three, Gunnar Gren, Gunnar Nordahl and Nils Liedhom, were the strike-force of Milan and became legends in Europe as the 'Grenoli' trio. Liedholm and Gren, with wingers Kurt Hamrin and Lennart Skoglund, were brought from Italy to form Sweden's attack in 1958.

Sweden were in all three finals tournaments in the 1970s, but missed out in the 1960s and 1980s. Manager Svensson took over in 1990, after their disastrous showing in the finals, with an early opportunity to prove himself, as Sweden were the hosts of the European Championship finals in 1992. Sweden had never been in the finals before, but now qualified as hosts. To their surprise, victory over England put them into the semi-finals. Although they were then well beaten by West Germany, Svensson had made his mark and self-confidence had been restored.

Tomas Brolin scored a marvellous goal against England and Jonas Thern was a key man in midfield, so Svensson wants them back fit and confident for 1994. Veteran goalkeeper Thomas Ravelli, with 100 caps, midfielder Stefan Schwarz of Benfica and centre-back Janne Eriksson are likely to be stalwarts, but it is the revival in form of the Borussia Moenchengladbach striker, Martin Dahlin, which excites the Swedish fans most. Sweden's Footballer of the Year, he is expected to help the team capitalise on their luck when they get to the USA.

* **Top: Sweden's 1993 Footballer of the year, Martin Dahlin, shows his paces against England's Des Walker.**

* **Right: Roger Ljung takes control during the 1-1 draw with France.**

SWEDEN'S RESULTS
EUROPEAN, GROUP 6

- 1-0 v Finland
- 2-0 v Bulgaria
- 3-1 v Israel
- 1-2 v France
- 1-0 v Austria
- 5-0 v Israel
- 1-1 v France
- 1-1 v Bulgaria
- 3-2 v Finland
- 1-1 v Austria

EUROPEAN GROUP 6
FINAL TABLE

	P	W	D	L	F	A	Pts
Sweden	10	6	3	1	19	8	15
Bulgaria	10	6	2	2	19	10	14
France	10	6	1	3	17	10	13
Austria	10	3	2	5	15	16	8
Finland	10	2	1	7	9	18	5
Israel	10	1	3	6	10	27	5

SWITZERLAND

The last time Switzerland reached the World Cup finals it was a disaster from the outset.

Left: Scotland's Ally McCoist struggles to make an impact against Switzerland's Andy Egli.

EUROPEAN GROUP 1 FINAL TABLE							
	P	W	D	L	F	A	Pts
Italy	10	7	2	1	22	7	16
Switzerland	10	6	3	1	23	6	15
Portugal	10	6	2	2	18	5	14
Scotland	10	4	3	3	14	13	11
Malta	10	1	1	8	3	23	3
Estonia	10	0	1	9	1	27	1

The night before their opening match at the 1966 finals three senior players were banished for breaking curfew. The next day the Swiss crashed 5-0 to a West German side inspired by a young newcomer named Franz Beckenbauer.

Now, 28 years later, Switzerland are back, serving notice that their country is not only the home of world and European governing bodies FIFA and UEFA but home to a rapidly reviving soccer culture.

As an echo of that last World Cup appearance, Switzerland's manager is an Englishman, Roy Hodgson, who has successfully mixed together the various elements of a Swiss culture which represents the German, French and Italian regional character and styles.

In goal is Marco Pascolo, whose talents Hodgson knows well since Pascolo, before transferring to high-profile Servette of Geneva, was Hodgson's protege at Neuchatel. In front of him is a defence secured by the veteran sweeper Alain Geiger, who will approach USA'94 with nearly 100 caps to his name.

Midfield is run by Georges Bregy, who thought he had retired from the international arena and had to be persuaded to bring back his particular strengths in both commanding a team and contributing to their fire-power with his abilities to turn the most innocuous-placed free kicks into goals.

But it is in attack where Switzerland, for years among the most goal-shy of international nations, are reborn. Three exports to Germany wield the power – Nurnberg's wide-running Alain Sutter, Stuttgart's tall but stealthy Adrian Knup (whose talents earned 11 goals in his first 12 internationals) and pin-up Stephane Chapuisat, from Borussia Dortmund.

The big Italian clubs were duly impressed with Chapuisat's displays in the qualifiers. Repeat performances in the finals would turn him into the most expensive Swiss footballer of all time.

• *Left: A miserly Swiss defence heads the ball out of the danger zone again.*

**SWITZERLAND'S RESULTS
EUROPEAN GROUP 1**

6-0 v Estonia
3-1 v Scotland
2-2 v Italy
3-0 v Malta
1-1 v Portugal
2-0 v Malta
1-0 v Italy
1-1 v Scotland
0-1 v Portugal
4-0 v Estonia

UNITED STATES

The United States have already won one World Cup battle before the tournament has even started.

THE MANAGER

BORA MILUTINOVIC

Born on September 7, 1944 in Yugoslavia
Appointed October 1991

They persuaded the rest of the world that a nation where soccer is not the pre-eminent professional sport has a right to host soccer's prestige event.

Now all that remains is for 'Coach Bora' (Bora Milutinovic) to convince his own players they can match whatever the rest of the world brings to USA'94.

The United States reached the semi-finals of the inaugural World Cup in Uruguay in 1930. But the American game gained much greater international exposure through the ultimately doomed North American Soccer League which attracted so many of the world's 'golden oldies', including Pele, in the late 1960s and 1970s.

Finally, in 1991, having obtained the rights to host the 1994 World Cup, the US federation made an inspired move by signing up Bora Milutinovic as national coach. Milutinovic knows all about World Cup management from his sucess in guiding hosts Mexico to the 1986 quarter-finals and then steering the unrated minnows of Costa Rica, astonishingly, to the second round in 1990 after sensational victories over Scotland and Sweden.

The present task has been immense because Milutinovic has had to manage two entirely different teams, both performing under the guise of Team America. On the one hand is the squad of 20-plus based at the World Cup training centre of Mission Viejo in California, made up of home-based players; on the other hand are the 20 or so Americans who have proved good enough to earn their professional soccer living in Europe.

World Cup goalkeeper could be Tony Meola – who starred in Italy in 1990 – while the centre of defence has been strengthened by the decision of German-born Thoms Dooley to take up the international option offered by the American citizenship of his GI father. Midfield competetiveness may depend largely on the Latin skills of Uruguayan-born Tab Ramos, who has played in Spain for the past four years. To score the goals Bora can look to two more 'Europeans' in the unpredictable, German-based Eric Wynalda and ball-juggling Roy Wegerle from English club Coventry.

It's a fair bet that many opponents will underestimate the professional experience available to the United States…and be in for a shock.

• Above: US 'keeper Tony Meola attempts to clear from Ireland's Eddie McGoldrick during a 1992 friendly.

ASPRILLA, Faustino
Colombia

Clubs: Atletico Nacional (Col), Parma (It)
Age: 24
International Caps: 10

Asprilla, a swift moving striker from Italian club Parma, is one of the most exciting players to have exploded on world football in the past 18 months. Parma gambled £1 million on this unknown in 1992 but he came up trumps by inspiring their run to the 1993 Cup-winners' Cup Final and Colombia's World Cup qualifying double over Argentina. Asprilla has signed a new contract to keep him at Parma until 1998.

BAGGIO, Roberto
Italy

Clubs: Fiorentina, Juventus
Age: 27
International Caps: 32

Italy's dreams rest with the Juventus hero who cost them a then world record £8 million when he transferred from Fiorentina just before the 1990 World Cup. Baggio's role in spearheading Italy's qualifying success and Juventus' 1993 UEFA Cup win was rewarded in December 1993 with awards as World Player of the Year (from World Soccer magazine), as FIFA Footballer of the Year and as European Footballer of the Year.

BERGKAMP, Dennis
Holland

Clubs: Ajax (Hol), Internazionale (It)
Age: 25
International Caps: 26

Bergkamp cost Internazionale of Italy £8 million when they bought him in 1993 from Ajax Amsterdam. Bergkamp is considered by many to be Holland's new Cruyff or Van Basten and lived up to the publicity by scoring Holland's decisive second goal in the crucial World Cup qualfier against England in Rotterdam in October 1993. He was runner-up the following December in FIFA's own Footballer of the Year poll among 70 national team managers.

BRATSETH, Rune
Norway

Clubs: Rosenborg Trondheim (Nor), Werder Bremen (Ger)
Age: 33
International Caps: 53

Bratseth has been playing sweeper for Werder Bremen in Germany since arriving from Rosenborg Trondheim in 1987. Twice he has been voted Top Foreigner in the Bundesliga and he was a key member of the Bremen side which won the European Cup-winners' Cup in 1992. A committed Christian, Bratseth runs a bible study group for team-mates and friends alike. He was once a transfer target for Manchester United.

CANIGGIA, Claudio
Argentina

Clubs: River Plate (Arg), Verona, Atalanta, Roma (It)
Age: 27
International Caps: 34

Flying winger Caniggia is expected to be back in action for Argentina at the finals even though he will only shortly have returned to duty after a two-year ban for failing a dope test while playing for his Italian club, Roma. Caniggia was one of the heroes of Italia '90 and his absence from the Final because of a ban – after being booked for handball in the semi-final – was a major factor in Argentina's defeat by Germany.

DAHLIN, Martin
Sweden

Clubs: Malmo (Swe),
Borussia Monchengladbach (Ger)
Age: 26
International Caps: 25

Dahlin, a powerful striker from Germany's Borussia Moenchengladbach, was voted Sweden's Footballer of the Year for his decisive role in the closing stages of the World Cup qualifiers. He began his career with Malmo and moved to Germany in 1992. He scored seven goals in nine games in the World Cup qualifiers and earned admiring glances from clubs in France, Italy and Spain before agreeing a new long-term contract with Borussia.

CHAPUISAT, Stephane
Switzerland

Clubs: Lausanne (Swz), Bayer Uerdingen, Borussia Dortmund (Ger)
Age: 24
International Caps: 32

Chapuisat, a left-sided or central striker, is the best of a string of successful Swiss exports to Germany, where he plays for Borussia Dortmund. Soccer stardom runs in the family: Chapuisat's father, Pierre, was a former international defender. His son moved to Germany initially with Bayer Uerdingen. Chapuisat's goals failed to save them from relegation but he impressed Dortmund, whom he then led to the 1993 UEFA Cup Final.

DIMITRIADIS, Vasilis
Greece

Clubs: Aris Salonika, AEK Athehs
Age: 28
International Caps: 25

Dimitriadis, attacking raider of champions AEK Athens, laid the foundations in the qualifiers for consideration as Greece's first World Cup super-star. Dimitriadis missed three of the eight qualifying matches through injury but has played well since being restored to fitness and manager Panagulias expects great things of him at the finals. Dimitriadis has been top scorer in the Greek championship for the past two seasons.

World Cup '94

KEANE, Roy
Republic of Ireland

Clubs: Cobh Ramblers (RI), Nottingham Forest, Manchester United (Eng)
Age: 22
International Caps: 16

Midfielder Keane cost Manchester United a club record £3.5 million from relegated Nottingham Forest last summer. At Old Trafford he is seen as the potential long-term successor in midfield to Bryan Robson. Keane began in Ireland with Cobh Ramblers and cost Forest's then manager, Brian Clough, next to nothing. He represents an exciting new generation of talented players who can keep the Irish among the World Cup elite.

GEORGE, Finidi
Nigeria

Clubs: Ajax (Hol)
Age: 23
International Caps: 11

George, a fast, skilful attacker on either wing or through the centre of attack, scored the decisive goal which earned Nigeria a draw with Algeria in their last qualifying match and thus a place in the finals for the first time. He plays in Holland for Ajax Amsterdam, whom he joined two seasons ago. Many leading Italian and Spanish clubs have already sent spies to report regularly on his progress in Holland.

KOSTADINOV, Emil
Bulgaria

Clubs: CSKA Sofia (Bul), FC Porto (Por)
Age: 26
International Caps: 43

Kostadinov, the greatest Bulgarian attacker since the late Georgi Asparoukhov in the 1960s, destroyed France virtually single-handed in the World Cup qualifiers. He scored both the goals with which Bulgaria won, against all the odds, in Paris – his last, crucial goal in a 2-1 win being struck with unstoppable ferocity in injury time. Kostadinov's success came as no surprise to his team-mates with FC Porto in Portugal.

MARADONA, Diego Argentina

Clubs: Argentinos Juniors, Boca Juniors (Arg), Barcelona (Sp), Napoli (It), Sevilla (Sp), Newell's Old Boys (Arg)
Age: 33
International Caps: 68

If Maradona plays, USA '94 will be his fourth World C after 1982, victory in 1986 and runners-up spot in 19 Since then he has been in all sorts of trouble with dru and the law and a string of clubs, including Italy's Napoli and Spain's Sevilla. Now back home with Newell's Old Boys he says he is a reformed character. The only question over his World Cup presence is fitness after experiencing a series of niggling injuries during his career.

MALDINI, Paolo Italy

Clubs: Milan • **Age:** 25 • **International Caps:** 48

Football runs in the family for Maldini, raiding left-back of Italy and Milan. Paolo's father, Cesare, was a sweeper who captained Milan to their first Champions' Cup success in 1963 and is now boss of Italy's under-21 team. Paolo began with Milan's youth section and made his first-team debut at 17. He has followed father's footsteps in winning the Champions' Cup and intends going one better by winning the World Cup.

MATTHAUS, Lothar
Germany

Clubs: Borussia Moenchengladbach, Bayern Munich (Ger), Internazionale (It), Bayern Munich (Ger)
Age: 33
International Caps: 104

Matthaus was not only West Germany's World Cup-winning captain in 1990, he was also voted Player of the Tournament by the world's media. Then Matthaus was a midfielder but last year he moved back into the role of sweeper. Bayern Munich's most influential player, Matthaus returned to Germany in 1992 after leading Internazionale to victory in the Italian championship and in the UEFA Cup. He missed the 1992 European Championship finals because of injury.

McGRATH, Paul
Republic of Ireland

Clubs: Manchester United, Aston Villa (Eng)
Age: 34
International Caps: 63

McGrath's presence at the heart of the Irish international effort during the past six years has been almost a miracle given the knee injuries which, over the years, have raised doubts about his career. He has stayed on his feet to establish himself as a stabilising force in defence and midfield for the Irish Republic. At club level, a transfer from Manchester United to Aston Villa revived his career.

MOLLER, Andy
Germany

Clubs: Eintracht Frankfurt, Borussia Dortmund, Eintracht Frankfurt (Ger), Juventus (It)
Age: 26
International Caps: 33

Midfielder Moller is the new superstar of German football and will be relishing the World Cup after inspiring the Germans' 3-0 victory over the USA in Miami last December. Moller was first spotted as a teenager by Berti Vogts, who was then Germany's youth boss. Vogts has long predicted that Moller will be Germany's playmaker at the 1994 World Cup. Moller made his name with Eintracht Frankfurt and Borussia Dortmund and now plays for Juventus.

OMAM BIYIK, Francois
Cameroon

Clubs: Canon Yaounde (Cam), Laval, Toulouse, Marseille, Lens (Fr)
Age: 27
International Caps: 62

Omam Biyik attained World Cup super-stardom in 1990 when he scored Cameroon's decisive goal in the 1-0 defeat of Argentina in the Opening Match in Milan. Omam Biyik was brought to France by Laval and has played in France for the past seven years with Toulouse, Marseille and Lens. Omam Biyik is a centre-forward with finesse and aerial strength who has emerged from the shadow of Roger Milla, his attacking partner in 1990.

World Cup '94

ONOPKO, Victor
Russia

Clubs: Moscow Spartak
Age: 24
International Caps: 19

Onopko, a powerful left-sided mid-fielder or left-back, is already the club captain of Russian champions Moscow Spartak. A former Soviet international, he made his debut as a substitute in a 2-2 draw against England. Onopko starred at the 1992 European championship when he was particularly impressive in direct opposition to Ruud Gullit in the goalless draw against Holland. Onopko was Russia's 1992 Footballer of the Year.

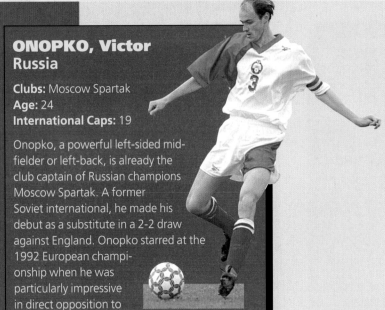

ROMARIO
Brazil

Clubs: Vasco da Gama (Brz), PSV Eindhoven (Hol), Barcelona (Sp)
Age: 28
International Caps: 46

Barcelona paid Holland's PSV Eindhoven £3 million last summer for the most lethal penalty-box poacher in the world game. Romario joined PSV Eindhoven after starring for the Brazilian side which finished runners-up in the 1988 Seoul Olympics. Romario totalled 98 goals in five seasons with PSV before his sale to Barcelona. He scored both goals in the decisive 2-0 victory over Uruguay which secured Brazil's ticket for the World Cup finals.

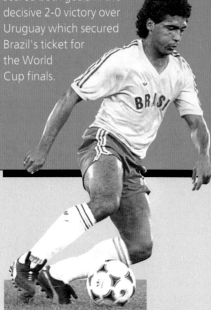

RADUCIOIU, Florin
Romania

Clubs: Dinamo Bucharest (Rom), Verona, Bari, Brescia, Milan (It)
Age: 24
International Caps: 22

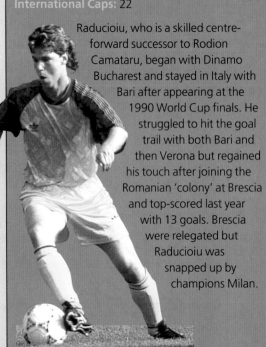

Raducioiu, who is a skilled centre-forward successor to Rodion Camataru, began with Dinamo Bucharest and stayed in Italy with Bari after appearing at the 1990 World Cup finals. He struggled to hit the goal trail with both Bari and then Verona but regained his touch after joining the Romanian 'colony' at Brescia and top-scored last year with 13 goals. Brescia were relegated but Raducioiu was snapped up by champions Milan.

SALINAS, Julio
Spain

Clubs: Bilbao, Atletico Madrid, Barcelona
Age: 31
International Caps: 38

Salinas, Spain's attack leader, has been kept on the substitutes' bench at Barcelona for much of this past season by Brazil's Romario. That only increased his appetite for goals and he scored a hat-trick in Albania and then two more away to the Irish Republic in Dublin to guide Spain through the gateway to the USA. Salinas began with Bilbao, joined Atletico Madrid in 1986 and then Barcelona two years later.

SANCHEZ, Erwin Bolivia

Clubs: Tahuichi, Bolivar (Bol), Benfica, Estoril, Boavista (Por)
Age: 24
International Caps: 34

Sanchez is the creative force who makes Bolivia's midfield tick. He started with the world-famous children's soccer academy of Tahuichi and was playing for the senior national team by the time he was 18. Sanchez moved to Europe with Benfica but took time adjusting and was sold first to Estoril then to his present club, Boavista. Sanchez scored vital goals for Bolivia on their way to the finals for the first time in 44 years.

SCIFO, Enzo Belgium

Clubs: Anderlecht (Bel), Internazionale (It), Bordeaux, Auxerre (Fr), Torino (It), Monaco (Fr)
Age: 28
International Caps: 62

Scifo, Belgium's midfield maestro, was born and brought up in Belgium of Italian parents. He opted for Belgian citizenship to make a teenage international debut at the finals of the 1984 European Championships. His talent attracted Italian clubs and he played for Inter and Torino as well as Bordeaux and Auxerre in France before joining his present club, Monaco. Scifo was a member of the Belgian side who reached the 1986 World Cup semi-finals.

VALDERRAMA, Carlos Colombia

Clubs: Millonarios, Atletico Nacional (Col), Montpellier (Fr), Valladolid (Sp), Medellin, Atletico Junior (Col)
Age: 31
International Caps: 57

Valderrama is nicknamed the 'South American Gullit' not merely for his frizzy hairstyle but for his attacking talents. Valderrama starred first at the 1987 Copa America when Colombia finished third. He was named South American Footballer of the Year and sold to French club Montpellier. Later came a spell in Spain with Valladolid before he returned home and regained top form last year with Atletico Junior of Barranquilla.

WEGERLE, Roy United States

Clubs: Tampa Bay Rowdies (US), Chelsea, Swindon, Luton, Queens Park Rangers, Blackburn Rovers, Coventry City (Eng)
Age: 30
International Caps: 14

Wegerle, Coventry City centre-forward, is one of the most international footballers imaginable. Through birth and parental qualification he had options of playing for England, Germany or South Africa but eventually threw in his lot with his wife's home, the US. He is a clever ball-player with the knack of doing the unexpected and his talent could make all the difference to an unspectacular host side.

ZAGUE Mexico

Clubs: Sao Paulo (Brz), America, Necaxa (Mex)
Age: 27
International Caps: 20

Zague, also known as Zaguinho or by his real name of Luis Roberto Alves, set a modern record when he scored seven goals in one international for Mexico last year against Martinique. Zague's father – who first bore the nickname thanks to his zig-zag style of dribbling – was Brazilian. He played with great success in Mexico to which his son returned to star in his own right after a teenage spell in Brazil with Sao Paulo.

World Cup

BOSTON (Left)
Foxboro Stadium

Stadium facts: Built in 1970. capacity 61,000

Distance: Foxboro Stadium is halfway between Boston and Providence, approximately 20 miles from the centre of Boston.

June/July weather: Average temperature 70.5F / 21.4C.

Attractions: Boston dates back to the American Revolution and is a cradle of American liberty. Boston grew as a harbour town and is still one of the nation's finest ports. The city is now a centre of banking and finance. Tourists can visit Boston Common, Faneuil Hall, the Swan Boats, and the USS Constitution. More than 20 colleges and universities are located in Boston including Harvard University, the oldest college in the United States.

DETROIT (Below)
Pontiac Silverdome

Stadium facts: Built in 1975, this domed indoor stadium will have natural grass in place for the World Cup. Capacity 80,435

Distance: The Silverdome is in Pontiac, Michigan, 18 miles from Detroit.

June/July weather: Average outdoor temperature 71F / 21.7C; average temperature inside dome 70F / 21C.

Attractions: In the 1920s the motor industry made its home in Detroit which became synonymous with the car and American manufacturing skill. In the 1960s, Detroit gave rise to the Motown recording label and stars such as the Jackson 5, Stevie Wonder and the Supremes. Today, the 1,000 acre Belle Isle Park attracts tourists with its beautiful beaches, a yacht basin, a zoo, an aquarium and a botanical garden.

ORLANDO (Below)
Citrus Bowl

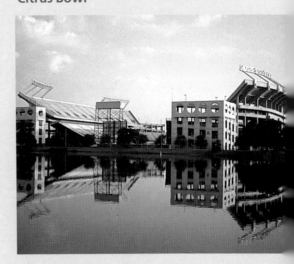

Stadium facts: Built in 1976, home of the annual Florida Citrus Bowl. Capacity 70,188

Distance: The Citrus Bowl is one mile west of the centre of Orlando.

June/July weather: Average temperature 81F / 27.2C.

Attractions: Orlando is the centre of one of the US' fastest growing areas. Famous for the world's most popular tourist attraction, Disney World , millions of visitors flock to central Florida each year. Epcot Centre, Disney MGM Studios, Sea World, Universal Studios Florida and Kennedy Space Centre are also in the area. Orlando has nearly 100 golf courses, tennis courts and many water sports to enjoy in the Florida sunshine.

CHICAGO (Opposite)
Soldier Field

Stadium facts: Built in 1922. Capacity 66,946.

Distance: Soldier Field is ideally located on the shore of Lake Michigan, south of the centre of Chicago.

June/July weather: Average temperature 70F / 21.1C.

Attractions: Housing major air, rail and highway hubs, Chicago has historically remained a centre of transportation. Tourists can visit the Museum of Science and Industry, the Field Museum of Natural History, the Chicago Art Institute and the Lincoln Park Zoo. Three of the five tallest man-made structures in the world give Chicago a world-famous sky-line. Chicago will host the Opening Ceremonies and Opening Match of the 1994 World Cup.

Venues

LOS ANGELES (Right)
Rose Bowl

Stadium facts: Built in 1922, famous for the Rose Bowl American football game held annually on New Year's Day. Capacity 102,083.

Distance: The Rose Bowl, in Pasadena, is seven miles from the centre of Los Angeles.

June/July weather: Average temperature 71F / 21.1C.

Attractions: By 1910, Los Angeles was already well known as the film screen capital of the world. The city has 46 miles of waterfront as well as a superb road network. Los Angeles was the home of the 1932 and 1984 Olympic Games. The town of Pasadena is famous for the annual Tournament of Roses Parade and the Rose Bowl American football game. The Rose Bowl will be the site of the 1994 World Cup Final.

SAN FRANCISCO
Stanford Stadium

Stadium facts: Built in 1921, the stadium of Stanford University. Capacity 86,019.

Distance: Stanford Stadium is in Palo Alto, 27 miles south of San Francisco.

June/July weather: Average temperature 59F / 15C.

Attractions: San Francisco survived a devastating earthquake in 1906 and thrives today as a major cosmopolitan city and a prominent transportation and industrial centre. More than 40 steamship lines use San Francisco as a port of call, importing merchandise from all over the world. Tourists can visit Fisherman's Wharf, Chinatown and ride historic cable cars. Palo Alto is a residential community with many parks, libraries and community centres.

DALLAS
Cotton Bowl

Stadium facts: Built in 1930, located in historic Fair Park, home of Texas' annual state fair. Capacity 67,600.

Distance: The Cotton Bowl is located in central Dallas.

June/July weather: Average temperature 83F / 28.3C.

Attractions: Located in the heart of northern Texas, Dallas boasts a broad economic base. Known for its production of oil and natural gas, Dallas also houses one of the largest inland cotton markets, thus the name Cotton Bowl. Tourists can visit the Dallas Garden Centre, the Dallas Historical Society Museum and the Dallas Symphony Orchestra. Dallas will be the site of the World Cup International Broadcast Centre.

NEW YORK/NEW JERSEY
Giants Stadium

Stadium facts: Built in 1976, home of the NY Cosmos soccer team 1977-84. Capacity 76,891.

Distance: Giants Stadium is part of the Meadowlands Complex in East Rutherford, New Jersey, about five miles from New York City.

June/July weather: Average temperature 74F / 23.3C.

Attractions: New Jersey boasts attractions such as Atlantic City and Princetown University. Known as the Garden State, New Jersey is famous for its extensive small-scale agriculture. New York City is just across the Hudson River from Giants Stadium, approximately a five mile drive. Tourists can visit the Empire State Building, the Statue of Liberty, the United Nations, Times Square and Central Park.

WASHINGTON D.C.
RFK Memorial Stadium

Stadium facts: Built in 1961. Capacity 56,500.

Distance: Robert F Kennedy Memorial Stadium is 20 blocks east of the U.S. Capitol Building in central Washington.

June/July weather: Average temperature 77F / 25C.

Attractions: The capital of the United States, Washington D.C. is filled with history and tradition. The monuments and museums are plentiful. Tourists can visit the White House, the U.S. Capitol, the Washington Monument, the Library of Congress, the Smithsonian Institution Museums, and the National Zoo. The Smithsonian Air and Space Museum is one of the biggest museums in the world. Washington is conveniently located near beaches and mountains.

World Cup '94

RESULTS

GROUP A

United States v Switzerland
June 18, Detroit

Colombia v Romania
June 18, Los Angeles

United States v Colombia
June 22, Los Angeles

Switzerland v Romania
June 22, Detroit

United States v Romania
June 26, Los Angeles

Switzerland v Colombia
June 26, San Francisco

GROUP D

Argentina v Greece
June 21, Boston

Nigeria v Bulgaria
June 21, Dallas

Argentina v Nigeria
June 25, Boston

Bulgaria v Greece
June 26, Chicago

Greece v Nigeria
June 30, Boston

Argentina v Bulgaria
June 30, Dallas

GROUP B

Cameroon v Sweden
June 19, Los Angeles

Brazil v Russia
June 20, San Francisco

Brazil v Cameroon
June 24, San Francisco

Sweden v Russia
June 24, Detroit

Russia v Cameroon
June 28, San Francisco

Brazil v Sweden
June 28, Detroit

GROUP E

Italy v Rep Ireland
June 18, New York

Norway v Mexico
June 19, Washington

Italy v Norway
June 23, New York

Rep Ireland v Mexico
June 24, Orlando

Rep Ireland v Norway
June 28, New York

Italy v Mexico
June 28, Washington

GROUP C

Germany v Bolivia
June 17, Chicago

Spain v South Korea
June 17, Dallas

Germany v Spain
June 21, Chicago

South Korea v Bolivia
June 23, Boston

Bolivia v Spain
June 27, Chicago

Germany v South Korea
June 27, Dallas

GROUP F

Belgium v Morocco
June 19, Orlando

Holland v Saudi Arabia
June 20, Washington

Saudi Arabia v Morocco
June 25, New York

Belgium v Holland
June 25, Orlando

Morocco v Holland
June 29, Orlando

Belgium v Saudi Arabia
June 29, Washington

* THE WINNERS AND RUNNERS-UP OF EACH GROUP QUALIFY FOR THE SECOND ROUND TOGETHER WITH THE FOUR THIRD-PLACED TEAMS WITH THE BEST RECORDS IN TERMS OF POINTS, GOAL DIFFERENCE AND/OR GOALS SCORED.

SECOND ROUND

C1 [___] v [___] 3rd
July 2, Chicago

C2 [___] v [___] A2
July 2, Washington

A1 [___] v [___] 3rd
July 3, Los Angeles

F2 [___] v [___] B2
July 3, Dallas

SECOND ROUND

B1 [___] v [___] 3rd
July 4, San Francisco

F1 [___] v [___] E2
July 4, Orlando

D1 [___] v [___] 3rd
July 5, Boston

E1 [___] v [___] D2
July 5, New York

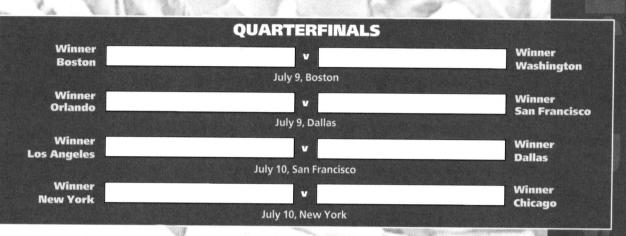

QUARTERFINALS

Winner Boston [___] v [___] Winner Washington
July 9, Boston

Winner Orlando [___] v [___] Winner San Francisco
July 9, Dallas

Winner Los Angeles [___] v [___] Winner Dallas
July 10, San Francisco

Winner New York [___] v [___] Winner Chicago
July 10, New York

SEMIFINALS

Winner San Francisco [___] v [___] Winner Dallas
July 13, Los Angeles

Winner New York [___] v [___] Winner Boston
July 13, New York

THIRD PLACE PLAYOFF

[___] v [___]
July 16, Los Angeles

THE FINAL
July 17, Los Angeles

[___] v [___]

63

World Cup '94 Competition

WIN 2 TICKETS TO THE WORLD CUP FINAL Plus A WEEK IN LOS ANGELES!

How would you and a friend like to be in Los Angeles for the Final of the World Cup? Enter our competition, and your wish could come true!

We will fly the winner and a friend to Los Angeles on 12 July 1994, where they will stay in a twin room for six nights (bed and breakfast) at the first class Radisson Hotel in Los Angeles. The package includes deluxe coach transfer from the airport to the hotel and from the hotel to the Rose Bowl, where you will have two tickets for the World Cup Final on 17 July 1994. You will also receive a souvenir World Cup Pack, and will return to the UK on l8 July 1994.

All you have to do is answer the three questions below, then fill in and cut out the entry form. Make sure you give your full name and address, and a telephone number. Send your entry to the following address, to arrive no later than 10th June 1994. The first correct entry drawn on 10th June will win the prize:

Dept KM, Reed Illustrated Books
Michelin House, 81 Fulham Rd, London SW3 6RB.

Conditions of Entry

1. This offer is open to customers who purchase Shoot World Cup '94. Photocopied entry forms will only be accepted with proof of purchase.

2. At least one traveller must be aged 18 or over.

3. Entrants are responsible for their own passport, visa and insurance arrangements.

4. Prizes are as stated and no cash alternative is available. The choice of time and place of departure and arrival and the choice of carrier are ours.

5. The decision of the judges is final. Answers to the competition and the winner's name will be supplied on written application.

6. Employees of Reed International Books Ltd and their families are not eligible for entry.

The prize is offered by Reed Consumer Books in conjunction with Sunset International Ltd, official FA-approved tour operators to the World Cup.

SHOOT WORLD CUP '94 COMPETITION

1. West Germany have reached the Final of the World Cup six times, but only one of their players has scored in two separate Finals. Who is he?

    (A) Gerd Muller
    (B) Uwe Seeler
    (C) Paul Breitner
    (D) Karl-Heinz Rummenigge

2. In the qualifying competition for the 1994 World Cup, which country conceded the most goals?

    (A) Faeroe Islands
    (B) San Marino
    (C) St Vincent
    (D) Macao

3. Rearrange these anagrams to find the names of two Englishmen associated with the World Cup win in 1966.

    (A) OOOBBBRYEM   (B) AAEMRSFYL